ROOKIE

SURVIVING YOUR FRESHMAN
YEAR OF COLLEGE SOCCER

BY DAN BLANK

ISBN: 0989697738
ISBN 13: 9780989697736

For Izzy… because one day it might be you.

TABLE OF CONTENTS

INTRODUCTION

A braham Lincoln once said, "Give me six hours to chop down a tree and I'll spend the first four sharpening the axe." Honest Abe knew that there's no substitute for preparation.

You are about to embark on one of the most incredible and memorable adventures your life will ever offer. You're about to become a college soccer player. Congratulations! It truly is a once-in-a-lifetime opportunity and believe me, it will go by much faster than you could ever imagine. Four or five years from now, a referee will blow a whistle and - *just like that!* - your soccer career will be finished. The game you love most will have vanished while the sound of the referee's whistle is still hanging in the air. You'll shout up to the heavens for just one more game, but it'll all be gone. And as you bargain with the gods for one more chance to wear that uniform and represent your college or university, you'll look back upon your four years and reflect upon all the things you wish you had done differently. You'll end up wishing that you could've known then what you do know now. You'll retreat to be alone with your sadness, and there in your despair, you will remember that quote from Abe Lincoln. And you'll wish that you had armed yourself with a sharper axe.

At least that's how it used to be. You on the other hand... well, you're different. You've chosen to prepare yourself. You've chosen to arm yourself with knowledge - *with some inside info* - and I commend you for it.

By reading this book, you've chosen to give yourself a head start and a competitive edge. Considering the world you are about to enter is predicated upon competition, any type of head start is a very valuable asset.

I've been coaching college soccer for more than 20 years. Among the many things I've learned is this: Freshmen struggle. Why? Because they're freshmen. Because they are inexperienced. Because they are dropped into a brand new world without the benefit of hindsight and the only way for them to learn is through trial and error, with plenty of error. I've spent two decades observing rookies making the same mistakes over and over again.

Yes, you're a rookie, but you don't have to be a bewildered one. You can give yourself a fighting chance to sidestep the landmines that have exploded beneath so many of your predecessors. Let this book be your GPS as you navigate your freshman year of college soccer, and you'll be thankful you did.

Here's the deal... It doesn't matter if you're a boy or a girl; it doesn't matter if you're going to a small school or a big one; it doesn't matter what division of college soccer you'll be playing; I'm going to give you a lot of excellent advice. You can choose to take it or leave it; that's entirely your call. But if you put your trust in me, I guarantee that your rookie season will go a whole lot smoother and that your chances of success will dramatically improve.

You're about to embark on the best four years of your life. Let's try to make them even better! C'mon Rookie, it's time to sharpen your axe.

SECTION 1
BEFORE YOU GO

1

Legacy

When you're planning your Spring Break vacation, what's the first and most important decision you have to make? Before you buy your plane ticket or gas up your car or pack your suitcase, you obviously need to pick your destination. Your destination has a major impact on all of the other choices you're going to make.

You have four seasons of college soccer. That's not a lot. When your career is finished, your coaches and teammates will talk about the kind of player you were; about the type of teammate and leader you were; about the type of student and citizen you were. The words they choose to describe you will be your legacy. Ultimately, on this trip that is college soccer, your legacy is your destination.

Before you start packing your suitcases, do yourself a tremendous favor and define your legacy. Figure out what your college career is going to look like. Find yourself an hour of quiet and solitude, and pretend that you are a college senior and your career has just ended. Looking back, what do you see? Over these past four years, who were you?

What type of player were you? What type of teammate were you? What were the principles that you refused to bend? Were you a leader? Maybe a captain?

3

What were the characteristics that defined you in the eyes of your coaches and teammates? Ask yourself, *"What will they say about me when it's all over?"*

Write it down. Write down your destination and keep it close to you. Refer to it often. Use it to guide your decisions on and off the field. Decide who you will be and how you'll be remembered and then live the life that you've envisioned.

Your legacy doesn't start during your senior season. Your legacy begins the moment you step foot onto that campus. And it's too important to leave to chance. Define the player and person you are going to be *before* you get to college. Pick your destination before you get in the car and go. It just makes better sense, right?

Leave a legacy that is worthy of you. You'll never regret it. I promise.

2

Goals

As you define and design your legacy, it's only natural that you will set some goals for yourself. Fantastic! You should have athletic goals and academic goals and goals for whatever else inspires you. Speaking from a strictly soccer standpoint, let me give you a few worthwhile goals for your freshman year. You can tweak them however you like and you are welcome to add others, but these will give you a running start.

- Make the travel squad for the first away trip. A little bit later you'll read about the tiers of a college soccer team, but for now let's just say that if you want to get in the game, you first have to *go* to the game. Being in the travel squad gets you in the hunt.
- Get on the field.
  Playing college soccer is a lot more fun than watching college soccer. Do what you need to do to get on the field. It may mean changing the way you play. It may mean changing your position. Stay flexible and do what you need to do to see the field.

- Be a great teammate.

  Be the type of teammate that you would like to have. Help your teammates before they ask. Do more than your fair share of the things that aren't as much fun.

- Earn the respect of your coaches.

  These are the folks who decide if and how much you'll play. Show them that you are someone who deserves to be taken seriously.

If you can reach these goals, then there's a pretty good chance that you'll consider your rookie season a success. If you win yourself a starting position right out of the gate, that's even better!

3

The Bubble

When I was seventeen, I couldn't wait to get out of my house and on to college! I was obsessed with the idea of sweet freedom – the chance to set my own rules and be my own person and drink from the cup of independence! College was going to totally rock! And believe me, it totally did.

If you have a similar outlook on college, let me tell you a little secret that I wish someone had told me: College is a lot smaller than you think, especially if you're an athlete.

College is a bubble. It's a sort of parallel universe that you get to inhabit for four or five years with hundreds or thousands of others, and regardless of how many others share your bubble, it's a bubble nonetheless, and that means all the inhabitants are in some way connected. And in that bubble, word travels, and it travels fast. Very few secrets survive inside the bubble. Remember that.

You are an athlete. That makes you high-profile regardless of the sport you play and regardless of the success of your team. You get to enjoy a certain double-standard. You'll get some free clothing and some nice meals and the chance to travel. You might even get an athletic scholarship. But most and best of all, you'll get to represent your university in the throes of competition. People will watch you and cheer for you. You'll be a celebrity inside that bubble. Plenty of people will know your name, and many people who don't know your name will simply refer to you as someone who is *on the soccer team*. *Soccer player* will become your identity. Some people will love you for it and others will dislike you because of it, but *everyone* will be talking about you if you give them the chance. This is the price of your celebrity.

Incidentally, don't kid yourself that the bubble only applies to schools of a certain size. I've coached at a school of 600 and I've coached at a school of 35,000 and I assure you, even big schools are small.

You have only one reputation and it is one of the very few things that is 100% yours. Take care of it. Protect it. Guard it with pride and honor. As an athlete you live at the top. The view from up there is much nicer, but the fall hurts twice as much.

And while we are speaking of your reputation, let me remind you that social media shrinks the bubble even further. Many college athletes will attest that social media is not your friend. From here on out, every status update you post or message you tweet represents far more than just you. You are now representing your teammates, coaches and your university. Something that is funny to you might not seem so comical to the athletic director or the university president. And once you put it out there, you can't get it back.

If you're having a bad day and need to vent, there's no law that says you must do so in a public forum. Have the maturity to exercise good judgment. The world doesn't need to know about every one of your perceived injustices, so find another way to blow off your steam.

There are parts of your life that are better kept private. Don't risk social media suicide because a week later you'll realize how stupid and trivial your declaration seems in hindsight. Coaches and administrators aren't very forgiving when it comes to social media, so handle it with caution and care.

We live in a time where everyone has a camera in their pocket. Keep yourself out of compromising situations and your worries will be fewer. Pictures of you dancing at a frat party won't do you any favors. When it comes to pictures, perception becomes reality. What actually happened takes a backseat to what appears to be happening. And just to give you a heads-up, if you're photographed holding a red plastic cup, your coach is going to assume that it's filled with alcohol. So will everyone else. That's just the way the world spins. It's an argument that you will never win, so you're better off just avoiding it altogether.

There are all types of landmines inside the bubble. Navigate them with care. In the end, you really just have to ask yourself if you want to be taken seriously as an athlete. If you want others to take you seriously, then you have to first take yourself seriously. In short, get past the party. The sooner the better.

4

Make Relationships

Imagine this: It's the opening morning of preseason and the very first thing you'll encounter is a fitness test. You'll stand on the goal line with teammates spanning out on either side of you. You look at the teammate to your left, then the teammate to your right. You realize that you don't know either of their names, yet here you are, on your first day of college soccer, competing against them for a chance to represent your university. Your entire day will be filled with moments just like this, competing against strangers – competing against fellow rookies trying to get noticed, and against returning players who are fighting to hold onto their positions and who view you as a threat.

It wasn't so long ago that the first day of preseason was like that for almost every rookie. Teammates were adversaries before they were friends. For plenty of freshmen, it still looks like that; but it doesn't have to.

In this book you're going to read a lot about returning players. Don't worry, some of them will become your best friends. But that's somewhere down the road. For now, let me tell you something very important about returners: They are incredibly territorial. If a player was a starter last year, she feels entitled to start this year. If she didn't start but the starter graduated, she feels as though she is entitled to that spot because she waited her turn. Your coach won't share those views on entitlement, but that's irrelevant right now, because all that returning player cares about is protecting what's hers like a Mama Bear. You're a threat, and when it comes to soccer, she'd just as soon kill you and eat you.

One of the best things you can do to help your own cause is to develop a friendship before you start competing against her. If you don't, then on the day you meet, you'll be meeting as adversaries. That's a tough foundation for building a relationship, and it's a tough way to gain acceptance into the team.

When preseason opens, you want to have some allies in the returning classes. You want some of those players to know you and to like you because they'll be your guardian angels and your passport. If they like you, they'll get you inside the club. I cannot possibly overstate how important this can be.

How can you build a relationship before preseason? Well, you can graduate high school early and enroll in the spring semester. I am not advising you to do this. Personally, I loved high school, so there was no way you could have talked me into leaving early and I would never try to convince someone to do otherwise. I'm just letting you know that it's a trend that has been growing over the past few years and it would meet the objective of establishing relationships well before preseason. If high school has lost its appeal, this is an option you may want to consider.

If leaving high school early isn't for you, how about enrolling in summer school? A lot of returning players spend their summers *in town*. You can take a class or two, earn a few quick credits and be left with an abundance of time to learn your surroundings and develop friendships with your future teammates.

Summer camps are another excellent relationship builder. Most college coaches run soccer camps and many of the players serve as camp coaches. See if the coach will hire you for a few weeks during the summer. Camp staffs tend to bond very well. There's something about trying to manage a group of 200 small children that leads to the birth of beautiful friendships.

If you can't get yourself physically connected to your teammates, then use phone calls, email and social media to build your relationships. Hopefully you spent the night with a player when you visited campus. Stay in touch with that host and the other players you met. You don't want to be a stranger when you step onto that field, so make the effort to stay connected.

I'm also going to advise you to do some reconnaissance. The internet is a valuable cheat sheet and you should use it to your advantage. Read everything you can about the team. Study the roster. Read the feature stories. Read every post-game article and watch every video. Listen to the interviews. You can learn an awful lot about your future teammates if you just pay attention.

When you show up to preseason, you want to know everything you can about the returners, starting with their names. Especially their names! Have those names committed to memory before you arrive. This will make your life much easier on so many levels.

And since you're doing recon anyway, pay attention to anything the coach says. If you just extract the coach's quotes from a season's worth of articles, you'll have a pretty fantastic idea of what the coach is looking for in his players and how he wants his team to play. This information is completely free. Take advantage of it. It's another great chance to sharpen your axe.

5

Preparing For Preseason

Preseason is an audition and no one lives under more scrutiny than the rookies. The returning players want to know what you have to offer and whether or not they should fear you. The coach has seen the returning players for at least a year, so he's got a pretty good handle on their abilities. But this is his first chance to closely evaluate you over an extended period of time, so he's going to watch you closely. I want you to take that as wonderful news!

You want to make preseason your showcase, and you want to give your coaches and teammates every reason to take you seriously, so let's start out with a few simple pointers.

- Juggle to 50

    I don't care if juggling isn't your thing; you're a college soccer player now, and at some point in preseason, you're going to be asked to juggle. Every college soccer player should at least be able to juggle to 50. You don't have to freestyle like one of those juggling savants on YouTube, but it also shouldn't look like you and the ball have never met. You're a college soccer player; that means you should be able to lift the ball off the ground *—with your feet —* and juggle to 50, end of story.

- Learn to do a proper push-up
  When the coach says, "Ten push-ups," for the love of Pete, don't do them with your knees on the ground. Learn to do proper push-ups, with your fingers pointing forward and your legs, back and neck straight as a beam of lumber. Don't just stay in one position and bob your head up and down like a chicken pecking at feed. Bend your arms to go down and straighten them to go up. You'll probably never be asked to do more than 20 push-ups in a single set, so train yourself to do 20 proper push-ups.

- Hire a personal trainer for a month
  You can figure out the push-up thing on your own, but when you get to college, you're also going to have to lift weights and do plyometric exercises. I highly recommend that you get some experience with these exercises before you have to do them in front of other people. Have an expert teach you the proper technique for squats and cleans and crunches and pull-ups and lunges and box jumps and all of those other magical exercises that you'll be doing in the near future.

- Develop your soccer IQ
  You can learn a lot from a book (maybe like you're doing now?). I seriously recommend reading *Soccer iQ*. Why? Because it will help you. I didn't write *ROOKIE* to plug my other books, but there's a reason that we make our team read *Soccer iQ* each year. Use it to identify and eliminate a lot of mistakes you're making and your chances of getting on the field will improve. I promise it will help you.

- Become a specialist
  One way to improve your brand and rise above the crowd is to develop a defining quality. As you work to develop all areas of your game, I highly recommend that you also specialize at something. Pick an area that you're already good at and become stupendous at it. Maybe you can become a set-piece specialist. Maybe you can add ten yards to your

throw-in. Maybe you can become a dominant header. Maybe you can learn to accurately smack a fifty-yard driven ball with consistency. It doesn't matter what it is, find something that you can be the best at and you will become more marketable to your coach.

- Have a clue about world soccer

Your universe is going to center around soccer people, so it helps if you can be conversational in their language. Stay informed. Keep up with the U.S. national teams and the Premier League and MLS. Know who the world's best players are and what teams employ them. If there's a World Cup coming up this summer, make sure you know about it. You don't have to obsess over this stuff, but at least have a working vocabulary.

6

You Belong

Preseason can be an extremely intimidating proposition. A lot of very good rookies crumble, and not because they lack talent. They crumble because they can't get their head right. They're so worried about disappointing their coach or pissing off their teammates that they never figure out how to present their best selves. They are so worried about being bad that they never get around to being good.

Listen to me: You belong! If that coach recruited you into his team, it's only because he feels you can make his team better. Make preseason a showcase of your best self. Make it a showcase of your talent and your courage and your aggressiveness. It may work out the way you like and it may not, but when preseason ends, you want to have a clear conscience about what you brought to the field every day, so don't leave any bullets in the chamber! Make your decision before preseason begins about the attitude that you will bring into it. You need to choose the player that your coaches and teammates will see on that field. Don't leave it up to chance; *decide* who you will be!

Will you make mistakes? Absolutely. Soccer is an imperfect game and you are an imperfect person. Don't dwell on those mistakes or I promise that you'll self-destruct. Coaches don't expect you to be perfect, so don't stress. Just do your very best with every chance you get. That's the only way you'll leave preseason with a clear conscience.

Yes, preseason is an audition and yes, a lot of eyes will be upon you, but that's just life and it's no reason for you to crawl into a shell. Use preseason to do more than just play soccer; use it to announce yourself! Use it as a platform to prove to your coaches and teammates that you are a player who deserves to be taken seriously and that yes, you do belong!

7

The Fitness Tests

The fitness tests... the three most dreaded words in college soccer. But since nearly every coach employs them, you're going to have to just accept them as a part of life and put your head down and grind them out.

Fitness testing is important to your coach for a number of reasons. First of all, if you can't run, you can't play. From a purely physical standpoint, fitness matters. Secondly, your fitness results say a lot about your commitment to doing what is asked of you. You are the only one responsible for your fitness and it is one of the very few soccer things over which you have complete control. To trust you, your coach needs to know that you'll do the work even when no one is watching.

The fitness test may be the first thing you do in preseason, before you even kick a ball; therefore it is the first chance you have to make a statement. If you have to run it anyway, you may as well run it in a way that shows you deserve to be taken seriously. Instead of lamenting your fitness test, you may as well just embrace it and use it to your advantage.

Now, since we can't make those fitness tests go away, let's at least make them more manageable.

In April or May you'll probably receive a summer fitness packet. Some packets are very detailed and will give you a day by day plan for your summer workouts. Your coaches put a lot of time and effort into assembling that packet and they created it to help you, so my advice is to follow it to the letter.

Among other things, your summer packet will detail the fitness test or tests that you will be expected to run. Your objective is to pass, and hopefully demolish, those tests when preseason opens. That won't happen by accident and it won't happen if you don't do the work. Let me be very clear on something: *You can't fake a fitness test.* Nor do you want to. Like I said, it is your first chance to announce yourself, so let's take advantage of it.

Here's another piece of advice, and it's one that you'll want to pay attention to even if you're already a fitness freak: Don't let preseason be the first time you run those tests.

Many fitness tests hinge on your ability to run at a proper pace. Let me give you an example.

The fitness test we run is called Man U. The players start on one goal line and the objective is to run 105 yards toward the other goal line in 25 seconds. Once they reach that line, they have 35 seconds to get back to their starting point. As soon as you fail to meet one of the time requirements, you are done. To pass the test, you must make 15 repetitions in the allotted amount of time. Here's the catch: The amount of time you have to run the first leg progressively decreases after the first ten repetitions.

For repetitions 1-10, you have 25 seconds to run the 105 yards. On repetition 11, that time decreases to 24 seconds. On repetition 12, the time decreases to 23 seconds and so on until on the 20th repetition, you have to run the 105 yards in 15 seconds.

It only takes a casual pace, basically a jog, to run 105 yards in 25 seconds. Once during preseason at Georgia, all the players were lined up to start the first repetition of Man U. The head coach yelled, "Go!," and the players began trotting down the field at a nice easy pace. All except for one that is. One rookie took off at an all-out sprint like she'd been shot out of a cannon! This player was pretty fast, so she made it to the line in about 12 seconds; meanwhile, her teammates were just crossing midfield. It didn't matter. Once she had run ten yards, it was obvious that she would never pass the test. No one on earth could maintain that pace. It was pretty apparent that this was the first time she had actually run Man U. She dropped out by the eighth rep because she had expended so much energy at the start.

The tragedy of the whole story is that the player was actually fit; she just didn't know how to run the test, so she failed miserably. Do yourself a huge favor and run the actual tests a few times before you show up for preseason. Learn the pacing. Being fit might not be good enough standing on its own. When the coach is administering the test, you've only got one shot at getting it right, so don't go in blind.

I recommend you run your tests in mid-May, just so you know what your baseline is and how far you have to go, then run them again every two or three weeks. That will give you the chance to experiment with adjustments until you have the pacing perfected. It's one more way to sharpen your axe.

Let me give you one other helpful tidbit. Every team has a player or two who excel at these tests. It'll be pretty easy to figure out who these players are because the returners will be talking about them before the session begins. If at all possible, line up beside one of these fitness junkies and use them to pace you. Hang right beside them for as long as you can and hopefully for the duration of the test. If they pass, you pass. Just remember, there's a reason they excel at those tests; it's because they are actually fit. If you want to keep up with them, you'd better be fit also.

8

The Commitment Test

I beg of you to pay attention to what you are about to read. I want to give you a sneak peek into the pyramid of urgency for a college athlete.

Right now, college soccer looks like it will go on forever. You get to experience four years of it, and four years might seem like an eternity. You probably feel that you can ease your way into it until you eventually hit your stride. That complacency puts you on the bottom of the pyramid.

On the other hand... Three and a half months after preseason opens, your senior teammates will see their soccer careers end. The thing they love to do most of all will be taken from them and they'll never be able to get it back. That means they have one last chance to shape their legacy, one last chance to accomplish everything they had hoped to accomplish as collegiate soccer players. Translated, that means they have one last chance to win championships. And that means more to them than you or any other rookie can possibly imagine.

That is why your fitness test results are just as important to your teammates as they are to you. From where you sit, your fitness test might be about how far you can run in 12 minutes; for the returners, particularly the seniors, your fitness test is about the *investment* you are willing to make to help *them* reach *their* goals. So, where you see a fitness test, they see a commitment test. And believe me, they are paying close attention to your results.

Do you know the saying that you never get a second chance to make a first impression? Well, the fitness test is the first impression the returners will have of you, and if you bomb it, they'll write you off before you leave the field that day. However, if you light that test on fire, they'll immediately take you seriously. They'll think of you as someone they can trust to help them get to where they want to be, and that will ease your path into the inner sanctum.

Don't ever give your teammates a reason to question your fitness. It's something you control, so own it! Please believe me when I tell you that from your teammates' point of view, the fitness test is not about running; it's about whether or not they can depend on you.

9

Make Your Own Decisions

E very team has its own chemistry and interpersonal dynamics at work. When you get to college, you're going to have a natural need to get information about your teammates and coaches. The returning players will be happy to give it to you, and often times you won't even need to ask.

When this type of information is being thrust upon you, take it with a grain of salt. The player telling you something is basing what she says on her personal experiences, and those experiences will differ from one player to the next. Just because someone is the first to tell you something, that doesn't mean her opinion is indisputable. My point is this: Be wary of the player who gossips and backstabs her teammates. She has an agenda and she is trying to recruit you to her side. She hopes to slant your view on certain people before you ever have the chance to know them. It is in your own best interest to avoid being dragged into any one clique. Stay open-minded. Don't let other people determine your relationships.

When a player backstabs a teammate, there may be a history there that you know nothing about. When she slams the coaches, it might be because she's been unhappy with her playing time. Whatever the motive, you're better off not drinking too much of her Kool-Aid. Just politely distance yourself from her as quickly as possible.

My advice is that you don't take anything too seriously on face value. Do yourself a favor and make up your own mind about your teammates and coaches. You may end up liking them or you may not, but make those decisions on your own terms and give everyone a fair shake. Four years later you'll be happy that you did.

10

Don't Burn Bridges

T his is one of those topics that you're much better off learning ahead of time. Here's the thing about college and college soccer… it might not work out, and there's a thousand reasons why. You might not like the academics. You might not like the social life. You might end up unhappy with your playing time or the style of play. You may end up not liking some of your teammates. And one or more of these factors may unsettle you to the point that you decide to transfer.

Now obviously we both hope that this isn't the case and that you are thrilled with your college choice and that your college soccer experience is exactly as you had imagined. But we're better off preparing for the worst and hoping for the best.

If you decide to transfer and continue playing college soccer, make no mistake, your coach is going to be a major part of your Plan B. You're going to need a release that allows you to speak with other universities, and your coach decides whether or not you'll get that release. Once you have a release, chances are that you're also going to need a recommendation from your coach.

The college coaching world is far smaller than you might imagine. I would bet that there isn't a college soccer coach in this country who isn't, at the very least, the friend of a friend of mine. If I don't know him myself, I know someone who does. Yes, we have a bubble of our very own.

When a player from another university contacts us about transferring to our university, the very first thing we do is call her coach and ask why she is leaving. And these coaches are brutally honest. They have to be, because in our bubble, what comes around goes around. We may be competitors, but we cooperate in these situations because we have to protect our names and because eventually the shoe will be on the other foot. My point is that your coach won't lie for you. He won't make you sound better than you are. He won't sugarcoat your abilities or the effect you've had on team chemistry. And, if the situation so warrants, he won't hesitate from telling us that you're a jackass.

The bottom line is that you need your coach, so even if you don't hit it off with him, do your best to maintain a positive relationship. If you're unhappy, don't go around lighting fires because you'll only end up burning yourself. Minimize your losses so if the time to transfer rolls around, your coach will be inclined to say nice things about you.

If you should decide to transfer, I strongly suggest that you inform your coach immediately once your season has ended. He'll want as much time as possible to replace you, particularly if you are on a scholarship. He might not like that you're leaving, but he'll appreciate the early notice because it gives him the best chance to find another player. In his eyes, when it comes to recruiting, every day matters. If you wait until mid-March to announce your intentions, you've left your coach with very little opportunity to find your replacement and he won't think so highly of you. And that's not the person you want talking to other coaches on your behalf.

If you decide to transfer, keep this in mind: At the moment you ask for your release, you basically cease to exist as a soccer player at your university. You won't be allowed to attend training sessions or other team functions. All of the resources you had at your disposal a day earlier will vanish. You won't even have access to a bag of balls.

I've seen players go through this and it's a little bit sad watching them search for other soccer opportunities around town, scrounging for pick-up games or kicking a ball against a wall. This is why, if you're set on transferring, I suggest you transfer at the Christmas break and start the spring semester at your new university on your new team. Hanging around won't do you or anyone else much good. You're better off making a clean break and getting your fresh start as quickly as possible.

11

Your Shopping List

You're going to think of plenty of things to bring with you to preseason. Excellent! Your room should be an oasis of self-sufficiency, and that takes preparation. When you've got an hour to nap between sessions, you don't want to have to run to the store to buy something you forgot. Let me give you a few things that probably haven't made your list but should.

Shoelaces — Everyone's shoelaces break somewhere along the line and it's never at a good time. If your laces snap when you're tying up your cleats for the evening scrimmage, you don't want to spend 30 minutes trying to find a replacement while the game goes on without you. Carry a spare pair in your soccer bag. As a matter of fact, carry two. Then you'll be able to help out a friend.

Febreeze — Spray down your dirty laundry with Febreeze to keep your room from smelling like the inside of your goalkeeper's gloves.

Dr. Scholl's Odor X Spray — It's Febreeze for your feet! Spray it on your feet to keep them healthy and spray it inside your cleats to keep them from stinking up your entire hallway.

A&D Ointment / Zinc Oxide Cream — There's an exceptionally high likelihood that you're going to experience a physical discomfort that I will politely refer to as *swamp butt*. And nothing is more irritating than a good old-fashioned case of swamp butt. A&D Ointment and Zinc Oxide Cream will get you back to normal pretty quickly, and you'll be very thankful that you brought them along.

Toilet Paper – When you have a case of swamp butt, that's not the time you want to discover that the dormitory toilet paper isn't quite as fluffy as you like. Bring a few rolls of your personal favorites just in case.

Cooler – You're going to need ice at all hours of the day and night. A cooler on hand will save you the trouble of hauling yourself out of your room or out of your building to reload your ice bags.

Ace Bandages – Use them to tie your ice packs to your body.

Pre-wrap – Because of its many functions, pre-wrap is like duct tape for soccer players.

Sun Block – You'll be outside 4-6 hours a day in August. Protect yourself. You've got enough to worry about; you don't need a sunburn.

Aloe – For those times when you forgot to apply your sun block. Keep it in your dorm fridge for maximum relief.

Lip Protection – You're going to be doing a lot of breathing through your mouth which can lead to a severe case of chapped lips. No fun.

Bug Spray – Nothing disappears faster during preseason than bug spray. Keep a can stashed away in your soccer bag for those times when the trainer's supply runs out.

Shoe Polish / Mink Oil – Preserve the life of your boots and help them keep their shape by shining them up each day. Shining your shoes is also a subtle yet effective way to show that you take yourself seriously as a soccer player.

Newspaper – When your shoes are wet, as they will likely be after each morning and evening session, the best way to dry them out is to stuff them with balls of newspaper. The problem is usually finding the newspaper. Bring some along with you and you'll be one step ahead of the game.

Two Alarm Clocks – That's right, two. As in plural. Why? Well, for starters, one might not do the trick. More importantly, if one fails, you have a back-up. Keep your alarm clock several feet from the bed. This will force you to get out of bed to shut that sucker off. Once you get to your feet, you're much less likely to fall back asleep.

SECTION 2
MEET YOUR COACH

12

Meet Your Coach

Meet your college soccer coach. He is not your club coach or your high school coach. This team is not something he does on the side to supplement the income of his *real* job. He has a mortgage and a car payment. He has a wife and 2.5 kids and a dog and all of them depend on him to pay the bills and put food on the table. Everything he does is centered on this one team. All of his energy is devoted to making this one team the best that it can possibly be.

His view of college soccer is much different than yours. Where you see the glory and the crowds and your picture on the website; he sees the paycheck he can't afford to lose. If you want to know why he's pissed off when you are thirty seconds late to a meeting, it's because he sees the big picture and therefore the little things matter to him.

He has a job and he wants to keep it. To keep his job, the one thing he absolutely must do is win soccer games. His fate is inextricably tied to the performance of a group of teenagers. Reread that last sentence ten years from now and you'll appreciate both the humor and agony.

Meet your coach. He serves many masters. In addition to the family that depends on him for survival, he serves a university that depends on him to set a good example; to play by the rules; to behave ethically; and to graduate players. And yes, this university depends on him to win games.

Meet your coach. He serves many masters and you aren't one of them. He'll do his best to look after you, to provide you with guidance and to keep you safe. He wants what's best for you, but not at the expense of what's best for him and his program. He has other masters.

Meet your coach. There will be days when you think he's an idiot. Rest assured that he feels the same way about you.

Meet your coach. He would love it if his team won *and* you were happy, but if he has to choose just one, well, you're out of luck. Remember, he has other masters, and the university really doesn't care if you're unhappy with your playing time. He is going to make his decisions based on one very simple premise: *What is in the best interest of my program?* Be prepared that you might not always enjoy his answer.

Meet your coach. He genuinely likes you and cares about you. He wants to see you do well. He'll do his best to treat you fairly and to help you up when you fall. He'll consider you family. He'll be sad when your career is over and proud on the day you graduate.

Meet your coach. There will be many days when you are convinced that you know better than he does. You do not.

Meet your coach. He will likely be the only college soccer coach you ever have. To you, he will always be one of one. To him, you are one of many; one of many who want more from him – more of his time, more of his approval, more of his favor.

Meet your coach. In four years, you're going to ask him to write you a letter of recommendation.

Meet your coach. No matter what you think of him, he is the one person you must please to get on the field.

13

Your Relationship

You're going to have some type of relationship with your coach, whether that relationship is close, distant or something in between. Regardless of the distance, you obviously want to have a positive relationship with the coach, so you can start by not making his life any more difficult than it already is. We'll go into some specifics later, but for now let me suggest that you strive to be someone that your coach will refer to as *high-trust, low-maintenance*. If you exist as a hard-working, responsible and dependable person who doesn't drag drama into his life, he's going to like you.

Some players want to have a close relationship with their coach, some do not. It's completely your choice and either way is fine. You don't have to have a close relationship to have a positive one. You'll get to know your coach and he'll get to know you just because you'll spend so much time together. I've genuinely liked plenty of players I wasn't necessarily close with, and I would imagine every other coach would say the same.

But some players want more from their relationship; some players were close with their club or high school coach and they want the same type of relationship with their college coach, or they want the college coach to serve as a father figure.

You can have whatever type of relationship you choose, however, understand that your relationship with your coach is up to you, not him. If you are a player that wants to be close with the coach, you'll be more than welcomed to do that, but *you* have to be the catalyst in that relationship. Keep in mind that *close* is a relative term and there are some lines that can't be crossed, and each coach determines those lines for himself.

There are a lot of eyes on your coach, and his objectivity needs to remain above reproach. Let's translate that to mean that your coach doesn't want people to think that playing time preference is given to the players he likes more than others. Therefore he can't actively seek out a relationship with you. If you want a close relationship, you'll have to go make one. Thankfully, it's really quite simple.

If you want a relationship that goes deeper than Xs and Os, then you're asking that your coach see you as more than just a player. For that to happen, you need to see him as more than just a coach. That's a difficult proposition if your only interactions are on the soccer field. To strengthen your relationship, start by doing some things that don't involve a ball and cleats, like popping by his office once in a while to chat about whatever is on your mind, and that shouldn't be limited to soccer. Let him get to know you on a personal level and he'll let you do the same.

When there's a team meal, don't be afraid to sit with the coaches if the seating arrangement allows. Most players try to physically distance themselves from their coaches at meals, and that's fine, too. But if the seating arrangement dictates that the coaches and players will share a table, pick a seat near the coach. The conversation at team meals usually doesn't revolve around soccer, so they provide an excellent chance for you to get to know your coach, and for him to get to know you.

There are countless opportunities for you to connect with your coach. Bus rides, hotel lobbies, fundraisers, community service and other non-soccer events all offer you a chance to build that relationship. But it's up to you to take the relationship to him.

Much like the whole of your college soccer experience, when it comes to your relationship with your coach, you'll get out of it what you put into it.

14

Slippery Slope

As you ponder the type of relationship you want to have with your coach, please heed this bit of warning: *Don't base your relationship on playing time.*

Remember when we said that you want your coach to see you as more than just a player? Well, that won't be possible if you base your relationship on how many minutes you get on the field. If you are going to be friendly when you play and antisocial when you don't, you'll never win your coach's respect. For your coach to value you as more than just a player, you'll have to value him as more than just a coach. That means you can't base your entire relationship on his game-day decisions about who plays where and for how long. If playing time is going to be the foundation for how you judge your coach, he is going to distance himself from you in a hurry. To have a positive relationship with your coach, you need to keep playing time in its own compartment.

15

Good Cop, Bad Cop

At some point during your college soccer career, there's a reasonable chance that you're going to wish that the assistant coach was actually the head coach. This isn't uncommon and I'll tell you why.

On most coaching staffs there is a good cop, bad cop dynamic. As the players see it, the head coach is the bad cop. The assistant coach is the good cop. Or Santa Claus. And everyone likes Santa Claus more than they like the bad cop.

At many programs, the assistant is the coach the players feel comfortable approaching with their issues. He serves as a sounding board to the players and an intermediary to the head coach. His role as a go-between is vital in ensuring that the players have a voice in the program. The players understand this and they like him for it. Plus, he's younger, cooler and better looking.

The big reason that the assistant coach always wins the popularity contest is that he doesn't have to make any of the truly difficult and impactful decisions. The assistant has the luxury of being closer to the players, because his objectivity isn't tested nearly as much as his boss'. The head coach needs to keep players at arm's length because he can't have his personal feelings interfering with his ability to make the difficult decisions that best serve his program. And ultimately, all of the tough calls fall to the guy at the top.

When I say that the head coach is the bad cop, I'm not implying that he is inherently mean, impolite, unlikeable, humorless or incapable of compassion. I'm just saying that a college soccer program is a business, and he's the CEO. He's got to make decisions that are in the company's best interest and those decisions aren't always easy and they aren't always popular.

It is the head coach who determines playing time, and that, in and of itself, will send some players campaigning for the assistant. The head coach also decides who gets scholarship money and who doesn't and what player gets more scholarship money than her roommate. The head coach decides who gets cut and just as importantly, whose best friend gets cut. If a punishment is doled out, it's the head coach doing the doling. This is no way to win a popularity contest.

These unpleasant tasks are all good and necessary to build a strong program, which is why the good cop, bad cop dynamic isn't such a horrible thing. Having a head coach that keeps a safe distance is good for you because it helps ensure that his decisions will be objective and fair and in the team's best interest. My point is this: Just because your head coach keeps you at a safe distance, it doesn't mean he doesn't like you or care about you. And believe me, if the assistant coach became the head coach, his days as the popularity contest winner would be numbered.

16

Choose Your Coach

Your college coach doesn't want to compete with other coaches for your undivided attention. The day you leave for college is the day you need to jettison your other coaches, and that may include your parents. Now I'm not suggesting that you completely eradicate them from your life, but you do need to eradicate them as your soccer advisors.

You're graduating into a whole new soccer life. To get on the field in this new life, there is only one person you need to please and that person is your head coach. He wants you to play a certain way. He'll explain his expectations to you and then it is up to you to rise up and meet them. It really is that simple.

Your former coaches may not agree with your new coach's philosophies or how he utilizes you or how much playing time he gives you, but none of that matters anymore because they don't run your new team. And any advice they offer that contradicts your new coach is detrimental to your chances of playing and developing as an important part of your new team.

Imagine you had to run a 50-yard dash against seven other competitors, but you had to wear a 40-pound backpack and the other runners didn't. That's what happens when you hang on to your previous coaches: They weigh you down and the other competitors pass you by. Now, imagine how much faster you would run if you got rid of that backpack. That's what happens when you release yourself from your former coaches.

You can only have one head coach. When you listen to voices that conflict with his, you are hurting your own chances to get on the field. You need to choose your head coach and say goodbye to the others.

If you're one of those players who can't let go of your previous coaches, you're going to struggle. Do yourself a favor and make a clean break.

17

He's Not Psychic

Don't expect your coach to know things that you don't tell him.

If you show up to practice in a funk and that negatively affects the way you're playing, there's a pretty good chance you're going to hear about it from your coach. Why? Because that's part of his job. Don't expect him to know that the reason you're in a funk is because your boyfriend is being a pinhead.

You are expected to live up to certain expectations. If there are mitigating circumstances that will compromise your ability to meet those expectations, then get out in front of the issue and let the coach know what's affecting you; otherwise he's just going to assume that your level of effort or concentration is substandard, and at that point you've dug yourself a hole.

Your coach may be a lot of things but he certainly isn't psychic. If you have a problem that your coach might need to know about, tell him. You can't expect him to know what's going on in your life if you don't actually share what's going on in your life.

18

Mind Your Pronouns

L et's do a little exercise in translation.

When a player says: "A lot of the players think that..."

The coach hears: "Me and my roommate think that..."

When a player says: "We all would like to..."

The coach hears: "I would like to... (and I hope some of my teammates feel the same way)."

When you approach your coach to speak about an issue, speak on your own behalf. Casually expanding your pronouns won't camouflage your agenda. Be an adult and say what you need to say. Have the conviction to present your case on its own merits instead of trying to fluff it up with support from phantom teammates.

I don't imagine you'll approach your coach very often as a rookie, but this advice will serve you well throughout your career.

19

Be On Time

If you want to announce your predilection for irresponsibility, show up late for team functions.

I don't know who first said that *on time means early*, but I'll bet it was a coach. Coaches are fanatics about getting things started on time. You need to know this going in.

The coach has a limited amount of your time, so he needs everything to run on schedule. He's also in charge of the team culture, so it's important that players show respect for the time of their teammates. When the coach says we'll meet at 10 A.M., he expects everyone to be in their places by 9:59.

When players are late, usually it's only by a minute or two. The reason players end up a minute or two late is because they didn't leave themselves enough margin for error. If they were supposed to be somewhere at 10 A.M., they tried to time it so they would walk through the door at 9:58. They didn't anticipate hitting every red light, or the accident that was blocking a lane of traffic, or that the hotel elevator would stop at every floor on the way to the lobby. When they encounter one of these surprises, all of the sudden their plan falls apart and they are late and the coach is unhappy.

Being responsible means being on time. You've got to allow for the possibility of unexpected delays and factor them into your plan.

If I'm scheduled to meet with the athletic director at 10 A.M., you can bet I'm going to be sitting in his lobby by 9:50. As the saying goes, *better an hour early than a minute late.*

I could find a thousand different ways to explain to you why it's important that you show up on time, or you can just trust me that it is. How about you just trust me on this one?

Incidentally, if you are going to be late, call the coach yourself. Don't ask your teammate to deliver the news because that just ain't gonna fly.

20

Deliver Bad News

Somewhere along the line there's a chance that you'll stumble into some real trouble. I hope that's not the case, but life happens. Whether that trouble involves your R.A. or your biology professor or the local police force, rest assured that your coach will find out. Remember that bubble we talked about? Yeah, he's going to find out.

In these moments, one of the scariest things you will have to do is tell your coach. Do it anyway and do it right away. Here's why:

First of all, your coach hates surprises. When it comes to problems of significant magnitude, your coach's boss, the Athletic Director, is going to end up being involved. Your coach wants the chance to tell the A.D. before the A.D. tells him. The coach wants the chance to say, "We've had this problem, I felt you should know, and this is how I plan on handling it." It shows the A.D. that the coach hasn't lost control of his program, and that's a big deal. When the A.D. knows about these things before the coach does, the coach looks less than professional and he doesn't appreciate the person who made him look that way.

Bringing the news to your coach also gives you a chance to control the story before all of the rumors start swirling around. There comes a time and a place to put all your cards on the table and just confess your sins. This is that time and place.

Finally, and this is important, you've got to give the coach a chance to help you. When you go into his office and unload your story, yeah, you'll probably have to face some consequences. But you know what, you'll survive them. What's far more important is that you give your coach a chance to be your ally so that you can face this difficult time together. If you don't recruit him as your ally, he may be left with no choice but to cut his losses and desert you. No matter what the problem is, you're much better off having the coach on your side, so get him involved sooner rather than later.

Coaches are programmed to take care of their players. You've got to give him that chance. When you go to him first and accept responsibility for your mistakes, it shows that you are putting your trust in him to take care of you, and that's going to help your cause.

21

Never Lie

When you report for your first season, you have several unblemished character traits, and one of them is your credibility. It will behoove you greatly to protect it.

Here's the thing… when you lie to your coach, you may solve a short-term problem. But if he ever finds out that you lied, your credibility is annihilated. And the chances of him finding out are excellent, *even if he never actually tells you that he found out*. Remember that you'll be living in a bubble, and word travels through that bubble with breakneck speed, particularly when a student-athlete is involved. For whatever reason, people *love* telling coaches about their misbehaving players.

Incidentally, word doesn't necessarily need to make it back to your coach for him to know that you're lying. Despite what you think, your coaches aren't idiots. They were once college students themselves and, as hard as this might be for you to believe, they still have pretty clear memories of those days. They know the types of situations you can get yourself into and they know the lies you might tell to save yourself. Most of the time they'll see right through your BS.

When you're sitting in the coach's office and the conversation is a tense one, I beg of you to tell the truth. At some point during that conversation, your coach is going to ask you a question about a possible indiscretion that you were a part of or aware of. Believe me when I tell you that he almost certainly knows the answer before he poses the question. He's just testing you. And if you fail that test once, you've failed it forever.

Since the day you were brought into this world your parents have been telling you not to lie. That's not by accident. They understand that the short-term consequence of telling the truth outweighs the long-term consequence of lying. You should take their advice.

22

Say Thank You

If you want to get college coaches into a frenzied conversation, mention the word *entitlement*. Coaches have a surplus of stories about players who feel they are entitled to everything they've been given and who keep asking for more. A disproportionate amount of what a coach hears can be translated to *gimme, gimme, gimme*. Believe me, it's exhausting.

Every coach enjoys a player that shows some appreciation for all that she is given. Show that these gestures and perks don't go unnoticed by occasionally saying thank you. Your coach will appreciate it and his opinion of you will rise.

SECTION 3
PRESEASON

23

It's A Job

"People don't play sports because it's fun. Ask any athlete; most of them hate it, but they couldn't imagine their life without it. It's part of them — the love/hate relationship. It's what they live for. They live for the practices, parties, cheers, long bus rides, invitationals, countless pairs of different types of shoes, water, Gatorade, and coaches you hate but appreciate. They live for the way it feels when they beat the other team, and knowing those two extra sprints they ran in practice were worth it. They live for the way they become a family with their team. They live for the countless songs they sing in their head while training all those hours. They live for the competition. They live for the friends, the practices, the memories, the pain. It's who they are. It's who we are."

— Anonymous*

Make no mistake about it; college soccer is a job. That will never be more clear than at 6 A.M. on an early August morning when you hear the alarm you could swear you set just five minutes earlier. As you roll over to silence that alarm, you'll feel a pain in your legs like nothing you've ever known, like a load of bricks has fallen upon them from three stories above. Your back and neck will be so stiff that you'll hear the vertebrae snap into place like ice cubes being twisted from their tray. You'll barely have the strength in your arm to reach that clock. You won't want to get up. The voice in your head will try coaxing you back into that beautiful sleep. It will tell you how much happier you will be if you just stay in bed. It will say, *"Just lay here for five more minutes. Trust me. You won't fall back asleep."*

No, you won't want to get up. But you will anyway. Why? Because this is your job now, and as painful as it might be, you know that it is the greatest job you'll ever have and you refuse to give it up just to stay under the covers. Welcome to preseason. Day Two.

College soccer will be much more demanding of your time than club or high school soccer ever was. In addition to your field sessions, there are team meetings and video sessions and road trips that last four days. There are tutors and study halls. There are sessions in the weight room. When you sign up to play college soccer, you are making a tremendous commitment, and at times this commitment can feel downright overwhelming. More than anything, it is this time commitment that leads us to define college soccer as a job. And three days into preseason, you'll understand the weight of that commitment.

How you position preseason is important. If you think of it as a week or two of physical and emotional misery, that's exactly what it will be, so let me give you a more useful outlook. Preseason is the closest thing to professional soccer that you will ever experience, so embrace it! It's the one time in your college life where you don't have to worry about going to class or meeting with your tutors or getting to your part-time job. During preseason, you are a soccer player, period.

Think of preseason as your showcase. You've spent months preparing; preseason is your chance to show everyone how hard you've worked while no one was watching. It's your chance to announce yourself as someone who has made the physical investment and is committed to bringing success to the program. It is your chance to show your coaches that you are a player who deserves to be taken seriously!

Is that going to make it hurt any less? A little bit. Maybe. Okay, preseason is going to hurt either way, but as the saying goes, *Pain is inevitable; suffering is optional.*

Do yourself a favor and have a plan for how you will approach each day of preseason physically and mentally. Predetermine the mentality you will bring to the field each day, even when your body is crying out for relief. It won't hurt like this forever. Make a decision about the player and person you will be, even when it hurts. Make a plan to be your very best self and then remember to stick to it.

I stumbled upon this quote online, and no one seems to know where exactly it came from.

24

Bigger Pond, Bigger Fish

My first college preseason was a long time ago, so most of the details have gone fuzzy. There is however, one moment that I recall vividly. It was the day we were handed our match schedule for the season. I don't remember that schedule because of the new opponents I was about to face, or because of the dates and times and locations of the games. Everything that I remember about that piece of paper was typed right there on the first line: *Men's Soccer Schedule*.

I had been playing soccer since the age of seven and playing for my school since the sixth grade, and in all those years, my greatest passion and the thing I could never get enough of was always referred to as Boys' Soccer. And now, this piece of paper delivered the news that I would never again play a game of boys' soccer. Now I was playing as a man.

When you were U-17, you played U-17 soccer. When you were U-18, you played U-18 soccer. The instant you step onto the college soccer field, you've just graduated to U-23 soccer. That's a gigantic leap! Everything you know about soccer is about to get bigger and faster and more physical.

There's a competitive pyramid of soccer. The bottom of the pyramid is based solely on participation and is crowded with very young, recreational players. As you got older, you moved up the pyramid and with each step of your climb, the pyramid got less crowded as fewer players kept climbing. Now, as you begin college soccer, you're very close to the point of that pyramid. Not many players make it to this level. The ones that do have shown some gift of talent and athleticism and the ability to adapt to the new challenges offered at each new step of the climb. You are one of those players. So are your teammates. You didn't get here by accident. And neither did they.

Meet your college soccer teammates. Every one of them was the best player at her high school or on her club. Yet some of them won't even make the travel squad.

You were a big fish in your last pond, but your new pond is much bigger, and so are the fish. Now you get to swim with the man-eaters.

You'll probably take some lumps in preseason. Things that worked really well for you against high school-aged players might not work as well against a 22-year-old senior. It's okay. Don't freak out and don't keep banging your head against the same wall. The way to survive in your new pond is to simply keep doing your best and adapting to the new demands.

Your teammates won't lie down for you. They aren't there just to make you look good. They're fighting to make a favorable impression on the coach... so are you! They're fighting for playing time... so are you! This time the fight is just going to be a little more difficult.

Remember, you belong here. Do your best. Don't ever quit. Fight like hell. This is your proving ground and everything you've ever done in your soccer life has led you to this moment. Stand up and make a case for yourself.

25

Your Best Self

The first season of the television show *Survivor* was won by a corporate consultant named Richard Hatch. Among his many claims to fame (or infamy), Hatch was the mastermind of *Survivor's* very first contestant alliance. He was reviled by the television audience for his willingness to manipulate the other contestants, but in the end, his deviousness was proven to be quite practical and it won him the million-dollar grand prize.

There was one clear difference that separated Hatch from the other contestants: Hatch went into *Survivor* with a plan. As a matter of fact, Hatch himself said he was amazed that, with a million dollars on the line, no one else had bothered to devise a strategy to win the game. While the other contestants were trying to figure things out on the fly, Hatch's plan kept him two steps ahead of them from start to finish.

If preseason is going to be your showcase, then you obviously need to showcase your very best self. It is my firm belief that, much like Richard Hatch, you are far better served by making a plan for preseason than by just showing up and trying to make adjustments on the fly.

Incidentally, I am not suggesting that you employ the same types of underhanded tactics that Richard Hatch utilized. As a matter of fact, I strongly advise you against tactics of manipulation because they will be counterproductive and your membership in your team will be short-lived. You are part of a team, whereas *Survivor* was the essence of *every man for himself*. That's a big, big difference. I only mention the *Survivor* reference because of its parallels to a college preseason, namely, a lot of people competing in a game, under difficult conditions, for a big prize and almost none of them having any clear cut plan.

Since preseason is going to have such a big impact on your soccer life, it's worth taking the time to formulate a plan. My advice is that you enter into a contract with yourself. If your preseason is ten days long, then that is the duration of your contract. Write out this contract several days before preseason begins. This contract is your plan and your commitment to showcasing your best self. I'm even going to provide you with the clauses of your contract.

- Train like a pro.
  As we've discussed, preseason can be exhausting. Doesn't matter. Remember this line from Alistair Cooke: *A professional does her best even when she doesn't feel like it.* You get to choose how you will approach each segment of each training session. Choose a great attitude.
- Under-promise and over-deliver.
  Don't burden yourself with additional expectations by announcing what you're going to do. Be humble. Be modest. Then go out and shock everyone.
- Outwork everyone, every day.
  This is the closest thing I can offer to a magic formula for earning playing time. If you are genuinely the hardest worker on a daily basis, your coach is going to find a spot for you. Like anything else, this won't happen by accident. If you want to be the hardest worker, then plan to be the hardest worker.
- Don't complain.
  Preseason is a wonderful breeding ground for complaints. It's hot. Of course it is. It's August. What did you expect? Your legs hurt. Of course they do. You're running yourself into the ground. What did you expect? When you focus on the things that bother you, you begin

to lose focus on the things that matter most. Don't waste your energy focusing on the things you can't control. The more you focus on them, the more they will consume you. Let your teammates do the complaining. The coaches will notice that you're staying above it.

- Be durable.

There's a difference between pain and injury and your ability to tell them apart can keep you on the field. Coaches know that preseason is painful for everyone. They notice and appreciate the players with the intestinal fortitude to tough it out. You will notice that many of your teammates will sit out some preseason sessions with *injuries*. Don't worry too much about them. You see, there's a great healing miracle that occurs every preseason: On the day before the first game or scrimmage, everyone is magically healthy again. Use preseason to show off your toughness and durability. You won't win a position by sitting on the trainer's table.

- Touch the line.

Be the type of athlete that you would admire. Whatever misery you must endure, attack it! Don't cut corners because that will just devalue your investment. Preseason only lasts for about a week, so you will survive. Give your best to it every step of the way. When the coach calls for a water break, jog off the field. When the water break is over, jog back on. When the coach calls everyone together in the middle of the field, don't walk to him; run. And when you are running suicides, touch the line with every single repetition. Why? Because that's what your best self would do.

- Use the fatigue of your teammates.

All of your teammates will be fatigued. There will be at least one session where the team moves about as well as zombie herd. This is a tremendous opportunity for you. When everyone else's level is going down, make yours go up. No matter how bad it hurts, force yourself to raise your level and you'll shine brighter than a diamond.

- Be low-maintenance.
  Don't reveal yourself as someone who needs to have a babysitter. Remember your equipment. Turn off your phone before team meetings. Get to everything on time. And for heaven's sake, take care of your injuries! When you get to college, treatment is not optional.
- Don't Coach.
  No one wants to be corrected by a rookie. There is nothing more annoying than a rookie who wants to coach her teammates. Your job is to do your best, not to worry about the shooting technique of your teammates. Communicate and compete, but don't coach.

Okay, so now you have some solid and practical ideas that you can use to establish your contract. If you polled all of the college soccer coaches in the country, I would bet that every one of them would tell you that what you just read is excellent advice.

Don't let preseason just happen to you. Have a plan in place and attack it!

26

Adapt

Preseason isn't necessarily just about the best players coming into camp; it's also about the players who adapt best to the new demands of the college game. Many high-profile recruits have been leapfrogged by a lesser-known player who did a better job of adjusting her game to meet the needs of her new team and coach.

Be prepared to change your position. You may have been a forward your entire life. Your college coach may ask you to play outside back. If that's the case, jump at the chance. You'll be much happier playing as an outside back than watching as a forward. Your job is to get yourself on the field.

A new coach means new rules and new expectations. Don't hang onto your old ideals at the expense of your playing time. Decide to be flexible and willing to adapt to your new environment. The sooner you adapt to these new expectations, the sooner you'll get on the field.

27

The Social Contract

When you join a team, you agree to accept correction from the coach.*
That is the social contract that you enter, and believe me, it is binding.
Your coach has a responsibility to demand the best from you, and he can't do
that silently. Everyone gets correction. Even you.

One of the best favors you can do for yourself is to be coachable. When the
coach corrects you, he feels he is helping you and that some part of you should
be grateful for having received this new nugget of wisdom. Coaching correc-
tions are not personal attacks, so don't take them as an attempt to embarrass
you in front of your peers. Your skin needs to be thicker than that.

When your coach is offering you correction, do not interrupt him to
say, "I know, I know." Seriously, he hates that. And his response is going to
be, "Well if you know it, why didn't you do it?" And that actually will be
embarrassing.

When your coach is correcting you, for the love of all things holy, do
not roll your eyes! That eye roll conveys the message that you already know
it all and that the coach is wasting your time when there are far better things
you could be doing with your life. Now, how do you think that will go over?

Listen to me... correction is a good thing. Accept it and grow from it. When your coach stops correcting you, he's stopped coaching you. When he stops coaching you, *that's the time to worry*... because your replacement is on the way.

I first heard this phrase from Bruce Brown, the amazing founder of Proactive Coaching. www.proactivecoaching.info

28

R*E*S*P*E*C*T

So far I've tried to give you the best possible chance of positioning yourself for a successful preseason that will hopefully lead to playing time and acceptance into your team. However, there is still one very large hurdle you have to navigate. To get a spot on the field, you're going to have to win it. That means you're going to have to compete and compete hard against your new teammates, including the returners. And that is where a good many rookies lose the plot.

There's no way around it; preseason is an awkward way to kick off your college career. In its strange dichotomy, preseason demands that you simultaneously cooperate with the same people you are competing against. You are locked into a mutual dependence. You have a responsibility to help one another, even while you are perhaps fighting for the same position. This can be a confusing time for a rookie, especially if you haven't yet figured out exactly what you want from your first year of college soccer.

Let me simplify this conundrum for you. Before you get to preseason, you've got to make a choice. You've got to decide what's more important: getting on the field or winning a popularity contest. If your top priority is to not offend your new teammates, plan on spending a lot of time watching college soccer games.

Yes, you will spend a large chunk of preseason trying to make your teammates look good, and you will enjoy doing that well. However, there will also be moments when you have to compete against the returners head-to-head, and that's going to have a massive impact on whether or not you get on the field when that first game rolls around.

Some rookies are so scared of upsetting the returners that they never get around to showcasing their best selves. The real shame of it happens weeks or months later when they realize that they are actually better than the players who are playing in front of them. When the duels begin, you need to have a clear conscience about doing your best to conquer your teammate/opponent, even if she's got some seniority on you. Remember what brought you to that program in the first place. I assure you it wasn't some odd fascination with watching your friends play college soccer.

The bottom line is that when it comes to playing time, your teammates are also your competitors. Now you can accept that and adjust to it, or you can leave yourself at the mercy of the returning players who have already learned that lesson. Seniority doesn't equal playing time, despite the wishes of the returning players. The best players play. Period.

If you want to play, there's only one person you need to please, and that is your coach. If you want his approval, I guarantee that you won't get it by continually deferring to the upperclassmen. You'll only get it by stepping onto the field and proving that you are the best player for the job. Accept the fact that you are going to have to fight for that position and that may mean ruffling some feathers in the process. But if you want the respect of your coaches and your teammates, you're going to have to go out there and earn it.

Soccer is a massive conglomeration of individual battles. You win respect by winning those battles as often as you can by as much as you can. Your teammates should not enjoy training against you. If your teammates enjoy training against you, you're doing something very wrong. On the other hand, if your teammates hate training against you, I'd be willing to wager that you're making a favorable impression upon your coach.

Now you don't have to take my advice. You are perfectly welcome to take the more submissive approach; just remember what you'll be giving up if you do.

There is one other really interesting tidbit that will turn this whole dynamic on its ear. It has been my experience that the rookies who come in and compete the hardest actually end up winning the popularity contest anyway. Why's that? Because they add value. You see, there's a core group of returning players that sit high up in the pecking order of your new team. When it comes to team chemistry, they steer the ship. Those core players have high ambitions for their team. They are secure in their roles as players and leaders, and because they wield so much power, they shape the team dynamic. And those players are thrilled when they see a rookie who is going to add value to their team. As for the rookies who show up timid, well, they are quickly dismissed as competitive assets. The leaders may genuinely like them as people, but they won't value them as players.

I once saw a television show where a law enforcement officer was teaching children how to react if someone attempts to kidnap them. His most memorable piece of advice was to put up your best fight before the kidnapper gets you into the car. He told the children that once the kidnapper gets you into the car, he takes control and your chances of survival are greatly reduced.

You need to think of the first day of classes as the car, because that's the day preseason ends. Once preseason ends, the shuffling of players naturally decreases as coaches make firmer decisions about their line-ups. Use preseason to put up your best fight and make your strongest case. You can make giant leaps in preseason; after that, it gets significantly more difficult to make up big chunks of ground.

Preseason is the hardest you will have to compete against your teammates because it is such a lengthy ordeal. You're basically cramming three weeks of training sessions into ten very tense days. Once preseason ends and classes begin, everything starts to shake out and everyone will calm down and settle into their roles. Once again, my point is, make your case in preseason. Put up your best fight when it will do you the most good. The social fallout you think you'll experience is far less than what you'll actually experience. Go out and earn their respect as someone who will help the team win. Do your very best from the very beginning or, believe me, you'll end up wishing you had.

29

Play To Your Strengths

I wish there was one magic formula for impressing your coach, but every coach is looking for something a little bit different, so there's no one-size-fits-all proposition. Your coach is going to have his own criteria and it might take you a little while to figure out what he's looking for. In the meantime, you've got to figure out how to make your strongest case as a player who will help his team win.

Before we move into what to do to win your coach's favor, let's talk about what not to do, and this one is in fact universal. If you want your coach to see you as an asset to his team, the one thing you absolutely cannot do is give the ball away any more than absolutely necessary. You have to show that you are trustworthy with the ball.

If you make 15 passes during a game, and 8 of them go to the opponent, your passing percentage is less than 50%. That means you passed the ball to the opponent more times than you passed it to your own team. In effect, you are playing for the opposition, and that won't help your cause. As a baseline for making your case, focus on keeping the ball for your team. Being dependable with the ball, in and of itself, may be enough to propel you into the top half of the talent pool.

However, you probably bring some other things to the table that you'll want the coach to notice, and preseason is the time to unveil those suckers.

The best on-field advice I can give you is to play to your strengths and away from your weaknesses. As over-simplified as that may sound, each year I see rookies who fail to put their best weapons on display.

If you are fast, then you need to look for opportunities to run footraces. You need to show off your horsepower every chance you get. When a teammate passes you a ball into space, sprint like an Olympian! If, on the other hand, you're not so fast, then you need to avoid those footraces whenever possible. You can't necessarily hide from footraces when it comes to your defensive responsibilities, but when your team has the ball, ask for it at your feet instead of into space.

If you are a 1v1 specialist, you'll have plenty of preseason chances to put those skills on display. Don't save them for a rainy day! Bust out your greatest hits as early as you can. And when you have the chance to go 1v1 at a defender during scrimmages or small-sided games, make the most of those opportunities.

If you specialize at taking free kicks or corner kicks, make sure you take some of them during your scrimmages. You may have to summon three seconds of courage to claim the rights to those kicks, but if you deliver, your stock can skyrocket!

Preseason may seem like an eternity, but at some point it actually will end. Make your best case as quickly as you possibly can. Give the coach a reason to notice you. If he sees something he likes, he'll see something he can work with, and then he'll begin looking for ways to mold your special characteristics into the framework of his style and system.

I once coached a player who had a 40-yard throw-in that nobody knew about until there was a week left in her rookie season. I coached another rookie who everyone thought was pretty slow until, with two days left in the regular season, she beat the entire team in a footrace. And I was left wondering, 'Where the heck has *that* been?'

Had these players unveiled their weapons earlier – *like during preseason* – they would have undoubtedly seen more playing time. But for whatever reason, they took the wholly impractical approach of hiding their special talents.

Don't make that same mistake. Do your best to play the game on your terms. Give the coach a reason to notice you and then make the adjustments as he coaches you.

30

Tell, Don't Ask

A t some point during training you'll be playing small-sided games, and because the numbers didn't work out quite right, your team will have a sub and the coach will leave it up to your team to take care of its own substitutions. He'll expect that every minute or two the sub will be rotated onto the field.

When you are the sub and it's time to get back on the field, you're going to be too scared to call a returning player off the field, so you'll opt to sub a fellow rookie out of the game. This might work once. It might work twice. But it won't go on like this forever. Eventually the rotation will dictate that you're going to have to cowboy up and pull a returning player off the field. If you're not a naturally assertive personality, this is going to be an uncomfortable moment and a tremendous test of your courage.

The players on the field don't want to come out of the game. The returners know that because you're a rookie, you're going to be pretty intimidated, and they are going to use that against you. You'll notice them mysteriously avoiding eye contact with you. This isn't by accident. If you're going to get them off the field, they're going to make you earn it by stepping up and showing some courage.

If you softly call out to the player you're trying to sub, she's going to pretend that she doesn't hear you. If you politely ask her if she wants to come off the field, she will politely decline. If you ask if she needs a rest, she will tell you no.

Now, you can spend a season learning what I'm about to tell you, or you can just trust me right from the start. In these situations, *Tell! Don't ask!* Muster up a half-second's worth of courage and forcefully *shout* out that returner's name! When she looks in your direction, just wave her off as you start jogging onto the field.

Will she love it? No. Will she get over it? Yes. In about four seconds. Why? Because she knows this is how the system works and she knows the system is fair. A minute later she'll be shouting at someone else to get off the field and it won't bother her one bit. It's all part of the evolution.

You won't win a spot by standing on the sidelines. Sometimes getting on the field means fighting your way onto it. If you don't want to spend your whole rookie season watching other people play, you've got to be courageous enough to sub yourself onto the field.

31

Targeting

This is the closest thing to a secret that I can offer you about competing for a position. If you're competitive and reasonably smart, you might have eventually gotten around to figuring it out on your own. I'm just going to use this opportunity to flatten out the learning curve for you.

Preseason can seem overwhelming based solely on the large number of people fighting for positions. It's pretty common to look at the herd of 25 players and hope to be one of the top 11. That type of thinking can devour you. Instead of worrying about the group of 25, we're going to focus on just one, single teammate.

Targeting is the process of figuring out exactly who you have to beat and then using that knowledge to motivate you on a daily basis. For example, if you're a left winger, and there are three other left wingers on your team, you try to figure out who is the best of the three and you focus on being better than that one player each and every day. Instead of worrying about beating out 24 other players or three other left wingers, now you're focused on outshining just one of them. It's a way to streamline your focus into bite-sized portions that are easily digested.

I want you to understand that I am not talking about anything underhanded. I'm not talking about sabotaging a teammate. I'm not talking about trying to physically damage one of your teammates or even wishing for her failure. I'm talking about using this one teammate as the measuring stick for your own efforts. Each day when you step on the training field, make it your mission to be better than that one player. Whatever she does, you do it just a little bit better. Wherever she runs, you run there just a little bit faster. If she quits after 99 push-ups, you make sure you get to 100. Whatever the case may be, make sure you are outdistancing her, even if it's just by one inch at a time.

Why does this work? Because it gives you a concrete model to measure yourself against. It gives you a living, breathing reason to perform at your very best each day. And it works because the player you target will have no idea that she's in your crosshairs. While she is motivating you, there's a good chance that no one is motivating her.

Now, since left wingers rarely confront one another directly during an 11v11 game, your opportunities to go against her head-to-head are limited to other drills and exercises. Chances are you'll spend more time trying to out-perform her than actually trying to conquer her in direct combat. That's why it's good to have a second target who will play opposite you. We'll call her your counter-target.

If you want to win the spot as a left wing, you've got to prove that you are the best attacking presence in that position. The easiest way to do that is to prove that you can conquer the best defender. If you've got the confidence to take on such a challenge, then your counter-target will be the defender that the coaches rate as the best. Try to find ways to match up against her whenever you can. When the coach breaks the team up into groups of four, five, six or whatever, try to get yourself into her group. Your objective is to match up against her in as many 1v1 duels as possible.

This probably sounds a little bit backwards to you, and believe me, I've seen a staggering number of players take the opposite approach. If they see they are about to be matched up against a very strong opponent, they'll find a reason to switch their place in line so they can duel against a softer opponent. Let me tell you why my way is better.

First of all, you don't back into great achievements. You're not going to sneak your way into the starting line-up. It's not like the referee is going to blow the whistle to commence the opening game and then the coaches are going to think, *'Hey, how'd she get out there?'* The Trojan Horse approach won't work in this environment, so you should abandon it before you get to campus.

Counter-targeting works for the same reason that targeting works: You have a reason to be inspired when your counter-target might not. While she'll still play hard and well – *she is the best defender for a reason* – you'll be playing with something just a little bit more. While she may be determined to play well, you'll be determined to beat *her*. Believe me, there's a difference.

Will this always work? There's no guarantee, but if you can consistently win your battles against the best defender on the team, your coach is going to notice and he's going to like what he sees in you.

Look, you're going to be matched up against that teammate countless times throughout the season anyway. You can't duck her all year. Why not just roll the dice and try your luck from the very beginning when making a statement will do you the most good? Proving that you can beat the best is an excellent way to get yourself on the field. And incidentally, this strategy works equally well for a defender who can consistently outduel the top attacker.

32

Don't Disqualify Yourself

When you're fighting for playing time, whether it's in preseason or beyond, the first thing you must take care of is ensuring that you don't disqualify yourself. The difference between you and the teammate you're competing against might be almost invisible. When it's time for the coach to decide who gets the spot, it might not be about the player who pulled ahead in the race; it might be about the player who fell out of it. Don't break the tie by getting careless.

Your job is to make the coach's decision difficult. When you break team rules or negatively affect team chemistry, you make his decision very easy. He's not going to reward you for failing to live up to the team's standards. I've said it over and over and I'll continue to do so: You've got to control the things you have the power to control.

Make sure you're taking care of the little things. Get to team functions on time. Obey the curfews and whatever other policies are in place. Don't lie or backstab your teammates. Don't doze off during a video session. And don't commit social media suicide. To win the race, you first have to finish the race.

There's no way for me to adequately stress the importance of not disqualifying yourself. I've seen talented players take themselves out of the equation year after year after year. It's happened on my teams, and it will also happen on yours. The good news is that you're now aware of it, so you can use it to your advantage. Responsible behavior will help you somewhere down the road. You'll read more about that later.

When it comes to staying in the race, don't underestimate the value of discipline. It's not just rule-breaking that can lead to your disqualification; a lapse in physical performance will have that same effect. You need to maintain your highest level of performance each and every day to stay on course to finish the race. Not all of your teammates will be able to deliver their very best on a daily basis. When their level of play drops, they fall off of the lead pack and a separation grows between them and the front-runners.

Let me put it to you another way. Think of every player on your team as a helium balloon. When you're all playing at your best, you're all bumping up against the ceiling. As a few of those balloons begin to lose some air, they begin to drop. They might not sink all the way to the floor, but they won't stay up at the same high level as the other balloons. The balloons that are up against the ceiling didn't get any higher, but because some of the other balloons sank, they look better by comparison. This is a fairly common phenomenon during preseason. It's not always about being the player that rises higher. Sometimes it's about not being the player who sinks. And what you do *off the field* will have a tremendous impact on the amount of helium in your balloon.

College offers you all types of freedoms that high school never did, and those freedoms will begin availing themselves to you immediately. Those freedoms will suck some of your teammates down the drain, and if you're not careful, you'll go down with them.

You have a preseason mission, and that mission is to prove to your coach that you belong on the field. Your climb is steep enough already. Don't make it any steeper by being undisciplined off the field. When you aren't getting enough sleep, your performance will suffer. When you are dehydrated, your performance will suffer. When you drink alcohol, your performance will suffer. Now I'm pretty sure that you already know all that; so what's the point in telling you something you already know? Well, despite your best intentions, your need for belonging can quickly lead to some seriously self-destructive behaviors.

It's important to remember that those 25 helium balloons are not clones of one another. Each one of them is going to be impacted differently, even when existing in the exact same environment. It doesn't matter if all 25 of you decide to stay up all night partying; the effects will be more damaging to some than to others.

I took up smoking in 11th grade. Why? Because I was an idiot. I thought that there was some void in my life that smoking would fill. I started smoking on a Wednesday, and I didn't just ease into it either; I went straight for the hard stuff – Marlboro Reds. By Friday night I had finished my first pack.

The next morning I had soccer practice with my club team and I was genuinely astonished to realize the devastating impact of my three-day habit! Remember that void I mentioned? Turns out it was my lungs. For 16 years I could run like a deer, but after one pack of cigarettes, I thought a soccer practice was going to kill me! I was literally starved for air! I remember struggling to run, gasping for air and thinking, *'Holy cow! All those commercials are right!'* It was horrible! Twenty minutes into that practice I decided to quit smoking. Forever! So you can imagine my surprise when I got to college and discovered that the fittest player on our team was a chain smoker!

My point is this: Just because everyone does it, it doesn't mean that you'll all fall equally. And since you don't know exactly how far you'll fall, and since it's in your best interest not to fall at all, I highly recommend that you avoid engaging in any behaviors that will be less than conducive to your very best performance.

Remember the story about Richard Hatch from *Survivor*? Well, this is another reason why it's so important to have a plan in place before preseason begins. This is why it's a great idea to have a contract with yourself. You need to make a ten-day commitment to focusing all of your energies into delivering your best possible performance, and a major part of that is going to mean saying no to some social opportunities.

The social life is going to sink some of your teammates, in preseason and beyond. Believe me, it will. If the person you are targeting wants to self-destruct, just stay out of her way. Let her create the separation for you. All you have to do is maintain your pace while she falls behind.

You have four years of college life. Don't try to cram it all in to the first ten days! As a matter of fact, you should commit to keeping those social opportunities out of your life for that first week and a half. Two weeks later you won't regret missing that party; but if you're sitting on the bench, you may very well regret attending it.

Not everything is under your control, but some things are. When you have the opportunity to control something that affects your performance, you've got to own it! Remember why you came to preseason in the first place. Be strong enough to sidestep temptation so you can make your best possible case. If you don't, you will most certainly regret it.

33

Three Kings

Let me introduce you to your three best friends for surviving preseason: Sleep, Water and Ice.

SLEEP - Unless you join the military, preseason is going to be the most physically grueling experience of your life. You're going to be tired – every day. You're going to be in pain – every day. And you're going to have to push through it and keep playing – every day!

You can't avoid the pain and the fatigue, but you can manage it. The better you manage it, the better you'll perform.

Sleep whenever you can for as long as you can. When you have three practices a day, an extra fifteen minutes of sleep can make a world of difference. Sleeping won't be the hard part; the hard part will be just getting to your bed. If you don't prioritize sleep, you'll find reasons to cheat yourself out of it.

When you finish lunch, instead of sitting at the table and socializing for an hour, socialize for fifteen minutes and then make a bee-line for your bed. Take advantage of opportunities to sleep whenever possible. You want to stay as fresh as possible to maintain your highest level of performance.

WATER - You'll probably never realize the impact that water has on your performance until you're officially diagnosed with dehydration. Water is the closest thing your body has to a magic potion. Proper hydration is extremely important, particularly in the heat of August. It will help your recovery; it will help your performance; and it will help prevent injuries and heat exhaustion. And as we learned in the last chapter, preseason is often a matter of attrition. If you're not hydrated, you'll never stay in the race.

A few days before preseason, you should start drinking water almost exclusively, and you should stop drinking anything with caffeine. When it comes to water, just drink, drink, drink! Drink even when you're not thirsty! Drink more than you think you need to drink! You don't need a reason, just keep drinking!

ICE - By now you've probably experienced a situation where a little knock that you took during a game is suddenly much more painful a day later. That's not some type of enigma. That's just how your body works. During preseason, you're going to be taking a ton of those knocks, some bigger than others, and if you don't treat them, they'll all hurt a lot more the next day.

If you've taken some lumps – even some small ones – get ice on them immediately after your session. You should spend a good bit of your preseason wrapped in ice. While water helps your body recover from the inside, ice is helping it recover from the outside.

If you have access to a cold pool, spend 20 minutes in it after every training session. If this sounds like torture to you, I really don't care. I'm not saying you'll enjoy it; I'm saying it'll be worth it.

Even if you maximize your opportunities to sleep, drink water and ice yourself, you're still going to be in pain. You'll just have to trust me that the pain you experience will be significantly less than if you hadn't done those things.

These are three things that are within your control. Don't be too lazy to pay attention to them.

Let me give you one other bonus tip that can be incredibly useful. If you are particularly stiff, sore or tight before a field session, pedal a stationary bike for 5-10 low-impact minutes to loosen up your legs. It'll do you a world of good.

34

Rites Of Passage

As a college rookie, you're a mule, particularly during preseason. You'll be asked to do more than your fair share of picking up cones and bagging balls and moving goals. Why? Because you're a rookie and being a mule is just a rite of passage that all rookies must endure. Every player before you has gone through it and a year later, you'll enjoy watching other rookies go through it too.

A surefire way to end up ostracized from your team is to skate these duties. It may seem silly or stupid to you, but to the players ahead of you, it is not. They served their time and they expect you to also serve yours. And your fellow rookies, well, they won't appreciate your disappearing act when it's time to do a little dirty work. Trust me, you're way better off just serving your time with a smile on your face than by butting heads with the system.

And since you have to endure these rites of passage anyway, you may as well use them to your advantage. Instead of just tolerating them, attack them! Do them with enthusiasm! Don't just pick up the cones; pick them up with gusto! Be the leader who gets the other rookies on board when it's time to do the chores. Your enthusiasm will be contagious, which will make the work more enjoyable. Plus, it will help establish you as a leader, and believe me, your coach will notice.

35

The Penal System

It doesn't matter how much the coach likes you, if you break a rule, there's going to be a consequence. There has to be. Why? Because coaches are forever concerned about setting dangerous precedents. When it comes to the standards of the team, everyone must be held accountable, and that duty ultimately falls to the coach. When coaches fail to hold players accountable, chaos quickly overruns the program.

If you stumble into a situation that involves some type of punishment, do yourself a favor and just take it like a champ. Don't stand there arguing your case. Just nod your head and say thank you and get on with it. And for heaven's sake, don't drag your teammates down with you. If Susie got away with one and you didn't, then so be it. Just swallow your feelings of grave injustice and accept that life isn't always fair.

Almost every player will have to endure some form of punishment before her career is complete. Do your best not to take it personally. Just get it done quickly — *and with dignity* — and move on to whatever's next.

36

Just Say No

Hazing is illegal and it's almost a thing of the past, but that doesn't mean that some teams don't still engage in it. If it's going to happen, it will happen during preseason. Don't put yourself at risk just to fit in with the group. If you end up in an uncomfortable situation, have the courage to stand up for yourself and walk away.

Your coach doesn't want the returning players hazing the rookies because it could cost him his job. If your older teammates attempt to haze the rookies, don't be afraid to notify your coach so he can put a stop to it. I know it's a difficult thing to do, but it'll be better for everyone in the end.

You're going to experience tremendous amounts of peer pressure in college. It'll be even worse for you because you're an athlete with a degree of celebrity. That makes you a trophy of sorts. When you arrive at college, you're expected to be old enough to know the difference between right and wrong and to act accordingly. Keep that in mind. It's not just about knowing what's right and what's wrong; it's also about the *action* you take.

Don't let other people, teammates or not, talk you into doing things you're not comfortable with. Be strong enough to stand your ground! Your peers will respect your courage.

SECTION 4
PLAYING TIME

37

The Four Tiers

When it comes to playing time, there are four tiers to a college soccer team:

- Starter
- Reserve
- Travel Squad
- Roster

The starters and the reserves are the players who actually get on the field on game day. The travel squad includes the players who make the trip to an away game but don't play. The roster players are the ones who aren't selected to make the trip.

There is a constant shifting amongst these tiers. Players are continually moving up or down depending on performance, injuries and suspensions. Making the travel squad is a very reasonable goal for any rookie who has joined a strong program. It means you're in the hunt to get on the field. When you aren't selected for the travel squad, you've got your work cut out for you.

It'll be pretty easy to know where you stand after a week or two of games. If you're a starter, then obviously you're doing something right. Just be aware that you do not own that spot; you are just renting it by the day. There are people on a lower tier who want what you have so you better keep working hard to defend it.

38

The Truth About Playing Time

Playing time is the currency of athletics. Your identity and your celebrity are inextricably linked to the number of minutes you spend on the field. Your coach knows that. And he knows the same applies to every one of your teammates.

College soccer is a cannibalistic frenzy for playing time. Everyone wants to graduate to the tier above, but no one is lowering a rope to lift up the teammates on the tier below. There's a lot of emotion tied into the prospect of playing time, but none of that matters when it comes time for your coach to choose a line-up.

Before we go any further, you need to understand that regardless of how good you think you are, you are not entitled to playing time. You're not playing club soccer any more. There are no more league rules that say you have to play at least half the game. Your parents aren't paying league dues. As a matter of fact, if you're on an athletic scholarship, the soccer team is paying you; that makes you an employee. You've reached a level where soccer is no longer about participation; now it's about results.

Only 11 players get to be on the field at any given time. Someone has to decide who the best 11 players are, and that job falls to the coach. It is his job to evaluate talent. Why? Because somebody must.

Remember, your coach has a job he wants to keep and that all hinges on winning soccer games. That means his decisions about playing time are going to be based on winning. He gives playing time to the players who he feels give his team the best chance to win games. If he believes you'll help his team win, you'll get on the field. Period.

If you're not getting the playing time you want from college soccer, the rest of this section will help you understand how to deal with your predicament and give yourself the best chance of earning more time.

39

You Don't Control Playing Time

Before you bury yourself under the stress of not playing, accept that you aren't the one who controls your playing time; your coach does. I know this is much easier said than done, but you've got to stay focused on the things you can control, and you can start with your effort.

Here's my advice: Focus on doing your very best and competing your hardest and outworking everyone each and every day. Don't focus on the end (playing time); focus on the process of becoming the best player you can possibly be. As you become a better player, your chances of playing more will improve.

When you focus on your playing time, you're burdening yourself with a lot of unnecessary stress. I've seen players so consumed with why they weren't playing that they completely ruined their college soccer experience and even took some teammates down in the process. Don't get tangled up in the things you can't control. It's a battle you'll never win and it will sap the life right out of you.

I don't know why you started playing soccer, but I know why you stuck with it; you kept coming back to soccer because it was fun. You enjoyed it so you kept playing it. Don't let playing time suck the fun out of this sport you love. You'll only hurt your own cause.

Playing time is first won on the practice field. You'll play better when you focus on giving your best effort and keeping the game enjoyable. Anything else you do will be counter-productive to your cause. Control what you can control and then hope for the best.

Sitting on the bench can be the most emotionally traumatizing part of a player's college soccer experience. You went to college to play college soccer, not watch it. You've never been told you're not good enough. You've probably started every game for every team you've ever been a part of, and now you're relegated to the role of spectator. It can be frustrating and maddening and all of that negative emotion can burn a hole through your stomach. I totally get it. But no matter the level of your anguish, you've got to find a way to manage it that will be in the best interest of both you and your team.

40

Your Teammates Don't Control Their Playing Time Either

I f you're one of those players who is going to obsess over playing time, prepare yourself to walk down a path filled with landmines. It won't take you long to pick a starter who you feel that you are better than, and she will become the target of your scorn.

Listen to me. It is silly and dangerous to be scornful of a teammate who is playing in front of you. Why? Because you don't decide your playing time and she doesn't decide hers either. If you're upset that Jenny is playing in front of you, don't blame Jenny. She's just doing her best because she wants the same thing that you want. It's not her fault. Jenny's not the *idiot* who can't seem to recognize your soccer genius; that *idiot* is your coach.

When you start dragging teammates into your personal house of misery, you become a cancer to your team and it won't be long before the coach decides his team is better off without you.

If you want to ignore my advice and make playing time your problem, then at least make sure you contain it as *your* problem.

41

Your Friends Will Lie To You

W hen you start campaigning to your teammates and friends about the playing time you *should* be getting, you're going to find a lot of people who agree with you. You're going to say that you don't understand why the coach can't see that you are so much better than Alex; and your friends will say, "Oh I know! You are totally better than she is!"

And guess what... they're lying to you. Why? Mainly because they love you and they want to support you. And also because no one wants to be the one who tells you that Alex is actually better than you. It takes a lot of courage to look you in the eye and tell you that the coach is actually right, and not a lot of people have that much courage in their tank.

Incidentally, if you start campaigning, remember that you are putting your friends into a very awkward position. By supporting you, they are betraying another teammate, and no matter what they say to your face, they won't enjoy being cornered like that. A player who takes her playing time campaign to her teammates will quickly become a major annoyance to those teammates.

Your teammates are all fighting their own battles. You can't expect them to passionately take up your cause as well. They want to play and they want to win and they want their team to get along. That's about the extent of it. Your battle is ultimately yours to fight and fight alone.

If you find yourself in this situation, it may be worth asking yourself why everyone is on your side except the coach. Is it actually that the coach is blind? Or is there just a small chance that maybe your friends are taking your side because it's the easiest way to keep the peace?

Look, it's difficult when you're not getting the playing time you think you deserve. Believe me, I know. But regardless of how badly it hurts, you've got to manage your pain with dignity. You've got to find a way to put the team first and stay loyal to the mission. You're all grown up now. By now you should know that life isn't always fair and that it doesn't always work out the way you would like. Even in the most difficult times, you've got to find a way to rise above your personal grief and present your best self.

42

Love Your Nose

There's another excellent way to disqualify yourself and it has nothing to do with team rules, but it has everything to do with attitude.

Let me make this impossible to misunderstand: Don't be a brat.

Yes, you may be genuinely disenchanted with your playing time and you may feel wholly justified in projecting that disenchantment, but when the spirit moves you to project, don't. Just don't.

There is nothing more annoying than a player whose body language screams, *"Look at how unhappy I am!"* Your coach knows that you really want to play, but that's not a good enough reason for him to put you on the field. For you to play, you have prove that you'll actually help the team win games, and you'll never do that by acting like a brat.

When the game ends, your attitude should reflect the team's success, not your own. If your team wins a game, the last thing in the world your coach wants to see is a player pouting because she didn't get to play. Yeah, it may be hard for you to control your emotions, but sometimes you just have to be a good actor. Sometimes you just have to put on a brave face and save your tears until you get into your car to drive home.

Of course there are other ways to pout, and you won't be the one to invent any of them. Disgruntled players will use all types of bad body language to express their discontent; they'll start mailing in their effort at training; they'll give the coach the silent treatment. Believe me, your coach has seen it all and he's gotten over it. Incidentally, few things will come off quite so foolish as complaining about your playing time when your team has just won five games in a row.

Look, when you project your personal misery onto the team, you're going to aggravate your coach and hurt your own cause. No coach is going to reward a player for acting like a brat. No one in his right mind wants to set that type of precedent! I've dealt with 23 years' worth of disgruntled players; do you honestly think I'm going to cave because you gave me your pouty face? Your coach is trying to protect his job and his paycheck and if that comes at the cost of your unhappiness, then so be it. This isn't rec soccer.

Somewhere along the line someone may have convinced you that the squeaky wheel gets the oil. Well, when it comes to college soccer, the squeaky wheel gets replaced. Coaches get paid to coach and win, not to babysit. It doesn't take a coach very long to decide that his team and his life would both be better off without a disgruntled player.

When you put your personal unhappiness ahead of the team, you'll just end up cutting off your nose to spite your face. Your coach holds the ultimate trump card and there is not a thing in the world you can do about that. You need to find a better way to make your case.

43

Positioning And
The Great Mistake

There are two ways to be a starter:

- Be the best player in that position
- Be the second best player when the best player becomes unavailable

If you are not a starter, it's because you aren't one of the best 11 players – at least not yet. This is not a time to panic and it's not a time to give up the fight. It's a time to give yourself the best possible chance to get on the field. In short, it's time to become the best of the rest.

I'm going to share with you a story that repeats itself each year at universities throughout the country.

After the first weekend of games, a loose hierarchy will have developed and players will have a fairly good idea of the tier that they inhabit. The problem is that some players forget that this hierarchy is not iron clad. They get so deflated after two games that they give up hope on the rest of the season. Immediately there's a noticeable decline in their training habits and their intensity level and they look nothing like the player who arrived at preseason full of excitement and determination. At team meetings, their minds are somewhere other than in the room. Everything they do says, "I'm just going through the motions." In short, they check out. And checking out is the great mistake.

You have to understand that a lot can and will happen in a college soccer season. The players who started the first game will not start every game, and there are a variety of reasons why. Some of those players will get injured or ill. Some will get suspended. Some will just get outplayed. These things happen all the time. The tier you inhabit doesn't have to be your permanent address. But if you're going to advance up the ladder, it won't happen by accident.

Instead of checking out, let's go the opposite direction and start thinking about *positioning*. Let's say you're an outside back, but you're not the starting outside back. The starter is the #1. That's her position and it will stay her position until further notice. You and the other reserve defenders are occupying spots 2-5. At that point, your top priority shouldn't be to win the starting spot – remember you don't control playing time; your top priority should be securing yourself in the #2 position. To put it another way, you want to be #2 and not #3, 4 or 5. Now, you don't want the #1 to get injured or to fail, but if something like that happens, you most certainly want to be the one who picks up the crumbs.

When you're not the #1, you've got to put your faith in the long haul. You've got to keep bringing your very best on a daily basis and hoping that your hard work will eventually get rewarded. You can't give up the fight after a day or a week or a month. If you want to eventually become a starter, then you have to train like one on a daily basis. It might not reap rewards as quickly as you like, but then again, it might. Either way, the coach is going to notice. He knows who the #1 is, but he is always making judgments about who will replace the #1 if circumstances arise.

Some of your teammates are going to check out. That's fine. It helps your cause. Just don't go down that road with them. Keep fighting for every inch, every step of the way, even when it feels like your effort is being wasted. When opportunity knocks, make sure it's you who gets to open the door.

44

Take The Answers

Here's the thing about your coach... He's sort of like a professor who has decided to feed you the answers to the next exam. That's literally what he attempts to do. Every day your coach tries to feed you the answers to a one-question exam, and the question is: *How do I get on the field?*

When you're trying to position yourself as the best of the rest, you've got to be smart enough to take those answers. It was actually a player who made me realize this.

In my current job, I am in charge of coaching the defenders at the University of Georgia. Every Wednesday night I meet with the defenders to review video of our most recent games. At certain points I'll freeze the video and ask the players, "Okay, what should happen next?" Or, "Where should this player be moving to?" I want each player to understand not only her position, but also the positions of all the other defenders. So I show them these situations and ask them to give me the answers.

A few years ago, during one of these meetings, I noticed that one player was answering the majority of the questions, and she wasn't exactly knocking people out of the way to do it. She would sit there and wait until it was obvious that no one else knew the answer, and then she would, almost regretfully, answer the question with absolute precision.

That's not the amazing part; the amazing part is that this player, Jenna Buckley, wasn't one of the starters. The starters could answer most of the questions, but not all of them. Jenna, on the other hand, could spit out the answer to each and every question I asked. This became a bit of a trend. Each week there was at least one question that no one could answer except Jenna. When I asked her how she always knew the answers, she said, "I just pay attention."

What a revolutionary concept!

I give my defenders a handbook that details our system and how to play it. I watch video with them at least once a week. And oh yeah, I work with them on the field. The questions I ask during videos aren't brain-busters; they are things we've covered time and time again. Every day I gave them the answers, but only one player was really paying close attention.

Jenna could have easily checked out. She wasn't starting and we almost never substitute our defenders. Jenna was a very talented player, but her chances of playing were slimmer based solely on her position. Still, she paid attention. And yes, she took the answers.

A few weeks later our starting center back got injured very late in a game. Jenna got to start the next game and she was absolutely sensational! Her understanding of the position was so remarkable that by the end of the game, Jenna Buckley was anointed as our new starting center back. Three months later, her teammates elected her as captain.

Jenna never checked out. Her training habits never dipped. She focused on the things she could control and did her best to own every single one of those things. And she paid attention. When I fed her the answers, she was clever enough to process and internalize them.

The coach wants to see you do well. He wants you to succeed. That's why he gives you the answers day after day after day. That's not by accident. If you want to ace the test, you've got to be smart enough to take advantage of his generosity.

And oh by the way, I hope you realize that I've been feeding you answers since you started reading this book. That's not by accident either. The question is: *Have you been paying attention?*

45

Your Most Abundant And Undervalued Resource

Y ou're going to have a lot of teammates, and none of them are clones. They all bring something decidedly unique to the table. They all have something that got them to the college level. And you can learn something from each one of them.

I've had the opportunity to watch fantastic youth players arrive to the college level and stagnate almost immediately. But I've also watched role players evolve into college stars due to a steady improvement in their individual games. It's remarkable how many of the players in the latter group began to resemble their more high-profile teammates in terms of their technical skill sets. Their 1v1 moves or the way they turned a ball or how they moved after a pass... it would often remind me of another (usually older) teammate. In a sense, they began to mirror the skill sets of the players who played the most minutes. Why? Because they saw something they liked from a teammate and decided to make it a part of their own games. Makes a lot of sense, right?

Someone on your team is going to have a phenomenal 1v1 move. Most of your teammates will say, *"Wow, she sure is great at that move! I don't know how she does it!"* You, on the other hand, can take a radically different approach and simply ask her to teach you how she does it. If you can master that move, you've just added one more tool to your toolbox and became a better player in the process.

To improve at a noticeable level, you have to do more than just show up. Yes, you will naturally improve simply by playing every day and adjusting to the new speed of play, but that's a slow climb. Wouldn't you prefer to accelerate the process? Of course you would! And you can! You just need to study the best things that your teammates have to offer and then learn to do those things as well as they do.

Your teammates will give you a buffet of choices for technical improvements. You don't need to reinvent the wheel; just take the best parts of everybody else's wheels! You'll begin to do this anyway without even realizing it. The key is to do it *while* realizing it! The key is to enter college soccer with the premeditated idea of borrowing the best that your teammates have to offer and incorporating those things into your own game. The more tools you can add to your toolbox, the better player you will be. And remember, the best players play.

Coaches aren't the only learning aids at your disposal. Pay attention to your teammates. Take their best ideas and add them to your game.

46

Charity Time

Despite what I've led you to believe, there are actually moments when playing time doesn't go to the very best player. Sometimes, when the score is out of reach and the result has been decided, the coach will have the luxury of giving other players their chance. Let's refer to these moments as charity time. And believe me, you want a piece of them! But before you have a chance to take advantage of charity time, the coach still has to pick you.

When the coach is deciding who gets the charity time, he's either going to choose the players he wants to see… or the players he wants to *reward*. If there's a tie between two players in terms of talent, he's going to pick the player he *likes* best. He's going to pick the player who has earned the reward by doing the right things, presenting a positive attitude and being a good, responsible teammate. This might be the time where picking up all those cones comes back to bless you.

Everything we've been discussing for the past several chapters has been about positioning yourself. Charity time is where all that positioning can pay off.

Understand that charity time will typically come in small portions, usually ten or fewer minutes. Doesn't matter. Don't feel as if you're above playing the final five minutes of a 4-0 game. Do not underestimate the value of charity time. Any amount of time is more than nothing and it gives you a chance to make a statement, no matter how brief. If you can string together enough of those small statements, you begin to make a real case for yourself.

Very rarely does a player go from not playing at all to starting in one swift motion. A starting position is usually won in chunks — one small chunk at a time. When charity time comes your way, make the most of it. For starters, don't take the field to maintain the status quo. Regardless of whether you are winning or losing, take the field with the goal of *changing the game*. If that game is a dying body, make it your mission to be the AED that shocks it back to life!

If you've been doing your work, you're probably 80-90 minutes fit. That's a lot of fuel to have in your tank for a ten minute performance, so don't pace yourself! Run around that field like you're riding a rocket! Your goal should be to empty your tank just as the final whistle blows.

When you're handed charity time, you've got nothing to lose! What's the worst that can happen? You're already not playing! Use your handful of minutes to showcase the turbo-charged force I know you to be! Believe me, if you buzz around that field like a runaway band saw, your coach is going to notice and he's going to like it and his trust in you will grow.

Charity time can be your chance to turn five minutes today into ten minutes next week into twenty minutes a week later and on to who knows what! Don't scoff at the opportunity. Take advantage of it!

47

Bass Player Wanted

Getting on the field is good; staying on the field is better! Let's talk about one excellent strategy for maximizing your minutes.

Do you know who Adam Clayton is? No? Well, I'm sure you've heard his music. He's the bass player for U2. You're probably more familiar with his bandmate, Bono.

Every band has its front man. He's the lead singer. His face is on the album covers. He's the one doing all the media interviews. He's the one the fans really want to see when they pay money to go to a concert. Bono is U2's front man, and since the late 1970s the band has been selling millions of records and making millions and millions of dollars. U2 has cemented its reputation as one of the greatest rock and roll bands of all time. And yet you've never heard of Adam Clayton. Strange, right?

Soccer teams operate with a similar dynamic. Each team has one or two or three stars. These are the players who create and score goals. These are the players that pay your coach's mortgage, so he gives them a little more freedom to freelance when the ball is at their feet. He lets them dribble more and shoot from odd angles and do some other things that he doesn't accept from the other players on the team. It's important to note that they were given these freedoms because they've proven themselves as stars; they didn't become stars because they were given these freedoms. Remember that.

To be good at your job, you have to know how you fit into the team. If you're a star, trust me, you'll know. If you're not (and 99% of us are not), it's okay. You can still be a great player and a vital part of the team's success without being in the spotlight. But you have to make peace with who you are and what your role is within your team. When you confuse who you are with what is expected of you, you're going to have problems.

Generally speaking, we ask our stars to win games for us. We ask everyone else to take the ball from the other team and then not to lose it. We ask that our non-stars play quickly and simply because when they don't, the other team takes the ball back. We ask that our non-stars pass to our team and not to our opponents. We ask them to defend like their lives depend on it. We want them to be ball-winners and distributors and to do the grunt work. We want them to do their job well enough that we have a chance to win the game.

If you're having trouble following me, watch some college or professional basketball games. The star is the guy who has the ball in his hands when his team is down by a point and there are three seconds left on the clock. The reason he has the ball is because he is the guy who is most likely to win the game for his team, and his coaches and teammates know that. So they give him the ball and get out of his way and let him do what he does best.

Imagine if by some miracle you ended up playing for the Miami Heat and your team was down a point and there were ten seconds left and you had the ball in your hands. At the top of the key, there is LeBron James with his hands out, begging for you to pass him the ball. But instead of passing to LeBron, you drive to the basket and your shot gets swatted down to the other end of the floor. Now, doesn't that seem idiotic? Of course it does! Why? Because LeBron is already surrounded by players who are much better than you – legitimate superstars – and even they know to get him the ball when the game is on the line.

Who you are right now is who you are. You have physical and technical limitations. Over time you will improve on those areas and maybe one day you'll become the star, but for now, who you are is who you are. And who you are today should dictate your role within the team.

Since you're not a star just yet, don't worry about playing like one. Right now your objective is to stay on the field. You do that by earning the trust of your coach. You earn his trust by playing your role, by executing your defensive duties, and by *being responsible with the ball*. I cannot overstate how important that last one is. You'll never stay on the field if you consistently give the ball to the other team. You need to show the coach that you're playing for his team, not the opponent's.

As you are fighting to make a case for yourself, let me give you some advice: When the ball is at your feet, do the simplest thing as quickly as you possibly can. The longer you have the ball, the more likely you are to lose it. Don't worry too much about impacting the score-line just yet; you'll have plenty of chances to do that when you're an established presence. For now, just worry about proving that you can be trusted with the ball. Keep it simple. Get the ball safely to your teammates on a consistent basis and your stock will rise.

That doesn't sound very glamorous, does it? No, it surely doesn't. But until you are a fixture in the line-up, you need to build your case one safe pass at a time. You won't ever be a star if you can't stay on the field. Right now just focus on doing your part to help the team win games.

What I'm trying to say is this: Don't be afraid to be the bass player. Not everyone gets to be the lead singer. Adam Clayton's net worth is roughly $150 million. Why? Because when the band sells records, the bass player gets paid too.

48

Feedback

If you're not playing as much as you like, I assure you it's not because the coach doesn't want his best players on the field. So the question that you need to ask isn't: *Why am I not playing?* The question you need to ask is: *What can I do to become a better player?* And the person you want to answer that question is your coach.

Periodically asking for feedback is a good idea, even if you're a fixture in the starting line-up. None of us are beyond improvement. And if you're not reaching your playing-time goals, then you have an even clearer reason for soliciting your coach's opinions. Your coach will be happy to offer you suggestions because your personal improvement is in his best interest.

When it comes to soliciting feedback, there are some things to keep in mind. First of all, you probably get feedback every day when you're on the practice field. Make sure you're improving on the things that have already been asked of you.

Secondly, there's a fine line between asking for feedback and campaigning for playing time. When you ask a coach why you aren't starting or why you aren't playing more, it doesn't matter what words actually come out of his mouth, the answer can be translated to: *Right now there are some players who are better than you.*

Instead of asking why you're not playing, try phrasing your query like this: *Coach, I'd like to try to earn more playing time. What areas do you think I should be focusing on to improve?*

Now, when your coach takes the time to answer that question, he isn't talking just to hear himself speak. Some players constantly ask for feedback as a way to feign interest in actually improving. If you're going to ask your coach for feedback, follow through by putting in the time and effort to improve, and that probably means coming out to practice early or staying late.

Let me clear up another wonderful misconception about putting in the extra time. Some players feel that if they set up an extra training session or two with the coaches that they'll automatically receive more playing time as a reward for putting in a few extra hours of work. That's not how it works. This isn't like turning in an extra-credit assignment to bring up your grade in history class. You don't train more to get more playing time. *You train more to become a better player.* When you become a better player, then your chances of playing more will naturally improve. Ultimately your playing time isn't determined by the amount of hours you log; it's determined by your ability to help the team win.

When your coach gives you feedback, he's done you a tremendous favor because again, he has fed you the answers. You have to be smart enough to capitalize on his generosity by putting in the right kind of work to become a better player.

49

Change The
Way You Play

At our end-of-season individual meetings, we inevitably have this conversation with one of our freshmen. When she was playing for her club, she was much more dominant than she was as a first-year collegiate player. That's only natural. At the club level she competed against players her own age and there were geographic restrictions on the available talent pools. When she gets to college, she is playing against players who are four years older and who come from all over the world. Even some of her fellow freshmen are just plain better than she is. The speed of play is faster, the game is more physical and the players are smarter tactically. She *shouldn't* be as dominant as she was in the club system. The things she got away with down there won't always work so well up here. But the biggest problem she faced came from her own brain because she refused to adapt to the demands of her new environment.

The jump from club/high school soccer to college soccer is immense. College soccer is a club soccer all-star game, and some of those all-stars have the benefit of two or three years of experience under their belts. You can't expect to waltz in and have everything work as well as it did when you were in high school. You should enter college soccer with the understanding that you're going to have to change some things about the way you play. You have to adapt to survive. It's soccer's brand of Darwinism.

You have strengths and you have weaknesses, and some things that were legitimate strengths in high school are now just average abilities in your new world. Speed is an easy example. Many who were the fastest player on their high school teams wouldn't finish amongst the top ten in a race against their college teammates. Remember – bigger pond, bigger fish.

You may have been a dominant 1v1 dribbler in high school or club, but guess what… you're trying to dribble against better defenders now. They're faster, stronger, smarter and as a bonus, they're going to be more organized. Don't expect college defenders to stand there like some of the cardboard cutouts you played against in high school.

By and large, the goalkeeping in high school soccer is fairly horrendous. If the ball gets on frame, it has a reasonable chance of going in, so players shoot from all types of ridiculous angles and distances and they're often rewarded with goals. Well, the goalkeeping is much better at the collegiate level so it might be a wise idea to give greater consideration to your shot selection.

These are among the most common issues that players are faced with when they get to the bigger pond. You'll figure out what works for you pretty quickly. You may have been the fastest player on your high school team and then find that you are also the fastest player on your college team as well. If you are, well then rock on! But chances are, when you get to college, some of your strengths aren't as mighty as you once thought.

Knowing your strengths is the easy part. The tricky part is letting go of the things that will no longer work for you. If you can't let go of those things, you'll just end up banging your head against a wall. Some things just won't work for you, no matter how hard you work at them. Sometimes hard work just isn't enough. Sometimes you're better off changing what you're working hard at.

You need to identify your new weaknesses. Accept your limitations and create a plan to reinvent yourself. Your ability to adapt will determine whether you stagnate or keep improving. If you stagnate, you'll see a flood of teammates passing you by in the quest for playing time.

At the end of your first season of college soccer, you should be able to definitively answer this question: *How have I changed as a player?* You should be able to produce some type of clear cut answer. In some form or fashion, there should be something different about the way you think and play the game. If there isn't, you are failing to adapt.

I guarantee you that your coach will have given you plenty of feedback on how he wants you to change as a player, even if you haven't asked for it. It's up to you to process that feedback and use it to your advantage to become a better college soccer player.

50

The Response

As we discussed, the tiers on a team are fluid. Players move up and down the ladder. Mostly we've been discussing how to get to the highest tier. But what happens when you reach that top tier and then get bumped down? This can be the most frustrating and emotionally charged experience of your college soccer career. Handling it with dignity is much easier said than done, so let's prepare your response before you're caught by surprise.

Telling a regular that she won't be in the next game's starting line-up is one of the most difficult things a coach has to do. But when he does it, you can bet that he's looking for a certain type of reaction from the player who was just relegated to the bench. Believe me when I tell you that the proper reaction to this adversity can go a long, long way in getting you back on the field sooner rather than later.

Earlier we mentioned that there are times when you're just going to have to be a good actor, and this may be one of them. When the coach gives you that news, swallow the lump in your throat, look him in the eye, and in the most sincere voice you can muster, say, "Ok Coach, whatever you think is best for the team." That's it. There doesn't need to be any more conversation and frankly, you probably don't want there to be. As soon as the coach says, "Thank you," turn and walk out of that room and find a quiet place to calm yourself.

In these situations, many players feel betrayed. I guess that's just natural because you'll inevitably feel a sense of ownership over a starting spot. You'll begin to think of it as yours and yours alone. However, as we've said from the very beginning, no one owns a starting spot; everyone is just renting, and that includes you. Moving players in and out of the starting line-up is just part of the business. And let's face it; when you were the starter, you weren't feeling sorry for the player behind you, so don't expect anyone to feel sorry for you either. Remember, your teammates all have their own battles to fight.

When the rug gets pulled out from under you, the worst thing you can do is give up hope. Not starting this one game doesn't automatically mean that you've lost the starting spot forever. Sometimes a coach will drop a player from the line-up just to send a message, particularly if that player has been dragging at training. The hope is to light a fire under the player and hope that she responds with enough fight to win back her spot.

I've seen many cases where the replacement starter had a horrendous performance and the position defaulted straight back to the player who had been benched. The problem is that you just don't know if or when things will turn back in your favor. So what do you do? You go back to positioning. You go back to fighting for the #2 spot.

I had a college teammate named Eduardo Ibanez who was a regular starter for our side. One Saturday afternoon, Eddie scored two goals, including the game-winner, in a game we won 3-2 over a national Top 20 team. When the coaches reviewed the video and charted the passing percentages of our team, they discovered that Eddie's passing percentage was 48.6. That meant Eddie had passed the ball to the opponent more times than he had to his teammates. Four days after being celebrated as the hero, Eddie was benched to start our next match.

When word got out that Eddie was going to be benched, his fraternity brothers mobilized and sprung into action. Forty of them showed up at the next game to heckle our coaches from across the field. They raised a giant white bedsheet with 48.6% painted on it, mocking our coaches for prioritizing passing percentage over goals.

No one knew how Eddie would handle it because regardless of his passing percentage, the guy had scored two fantastic goals and won the game for us. That wouldn't sit very well with most folks. Not many of Eddie's teammates would blame him if he didn't have the world's greatest attitude while he was sitting on the bench, and having an entire fraternity loudly chanting about this injustice would only give him more of a reason to explode. And explode he did.

From the moment the referee blew the whistle to start the game, Eddie was on his feet, waving a towel, and screaming his head off in support of the teammate who had taken his spot. Eddie had morphed into the most vocal supporter our team had ever known. He was relentless in his support of the entire team for the entire game. It was literally inspiring to see what a stand-up guy my friend truly was.

It's easy to be positive when things are going your way, but the measure of any person is found in how he or she responds to adversity. Despite the injustice that many perceived, Eddie remained loyal to his teammates, coaches and the mission. Eddie's display not only showcased him as a teammate we would all want, but it also positioned him as a player the coaches wouldn't mind putting back on the field.

Eddie's role as a reserve didn't last but a game or two. He won back his spot pretty quickly and his soccer life got back to the way he wanted it, but we can learn a lot from Eddie's day on the bench. You see, when you're faced with challenging situations, all that's left to do is choose how you will respond to them. Eddie's response was both courageous and remarkable and it showcased his very best self.

If you are ever faced with this same predicament, I recommend you do the same.

SECTION 5
TEAM CULTURE

51

It's Chemical

Team chemistry is impossible to measure and also impossible to miss. It is a vital part of any successful college soccer program. It's very difficult to battle your opponents when you're constantly stopping to battle yourself. Good chemistry can take a team to unbelievable heights, while bad chemistry can dismantle the most talented team.

Team chemistry is an undeniable factor in the success of any program, and it's everyone's job to protect it. Even you, Rookie.

You'll hear this many more times before your career is finished, but once you join that college soccer team, your actions affect far more than just you. Try to remember that when you're toying with the idea of doing something incredibly stupid. When your recklessness negatively affects the team, you become a chemistry problem.

52

Cat And Mouse

When you play club or high school soccer, there tends to be a cat and mouse arrangement with the rules. The coach is the cat and the players are all mice and the rules only matter if the coach catches you breaking them. That won't be the case when you join a college program that takes itself seriously. In a college program with a strong culture, everyone is responsible for guarding the cheese.

You aren't stepping into a team; you're stepping into a culture. In this culture, the rules matter. They matter to your coaches and yes, they even matter to your teammates. Chances are, your teammates had a hand in setting up the rules and the standards that govern this culture and they are proud of them.

You see, you're just a rookie and college looks like a place of infinite possibilities where you can cut loose and run wide open. But remember those seniors we talked about way back when? This is their last chance to do something fantastic as soccer players. This is their last chance to shine up their legacies, and that is very important to them. And they understand the value of the rules. They understand that the rules and standards exist for a reason and that the team is better when everyone is living up to those standards. And they sure as heck don't appreciate a stupid rookie screwing around with their last season of college soccer. When you break the rules of your college soccer program, it won't be just the coach who comes gunning for you. Your willingness to submit to the culture will have a bigger effect on your team's chemistry than you probably imagine.

Whatever culture exists around your program, your first semester is not the time to challenge it. Your rookie season is your time to embrace this new culture and simply accept it until you eventually grow to understand it. All of the silly things you don't understand exist for a reason and eventually those reasons will unveil themselves to you. And when they do, and you come to appreciate them, you'll find yourself defending them and imparting them onto a new class of rookies. Until that day arrives, put your faith in your program and trust that there are very good reasons for the things you don't yet understand.

53

No Backstabbing

If you want your teammates to ostracize you in a hurry, here's a foolproof recipe: Talk badly about them behind their backs.

To be honest, I'm not really sure if it's such a good idea to even include this chapter because if you're not a person who backstabs your teammates, you don't need to read it. And if you are that type of person, I doubt that reading this book is going to save you. But I'm going to include it anyway, if for no other reason than maybe it will give you the courage to confront a teammate who begins to backstab other teammates.

Team chemistry hinges on the ability of teammates to trust one another. That will never happen when players are worried about what's being said when they aren't in the room. Incidentally, just so we are crystal clear about this, when you speak badly about a teammate behind her back, she absolutely will find out about it. Believe it! And when she does, then you've got some real problems. And chances are your team does too.

To have great teammates, you've first got to be a great teammate. For teammates to protect you, you have to be willing to protect them. Instead of slamming your teammates when they aren't around, make it your goal to protect them instead. Don't tolerate it when others start badmouthing your teammates.

Don't be afraid to stand up and say, "Hey, so and so is a friend of mine and I don't appreciate you talking behind her back like this."

Yeah, it's difficult to have the courage to stand up to anyone in a situation like this, particularly a teammate, but if you do, word will get around that you're a stand-up teammate and your street credit will go through the roof.

54

Baggage

Soccer practice is not the place to drag your personal baggage. You and all of your teammates have plenty of battles to fight off the soccer field. You've all got to deal with academic challenges and relationship issues and car troubles and the many other landmines that make up the college experience. The soccer field should be a sanctuary from all of that baggage for you *and* your teammates. Soccer practice should be the favorite part of your day. You should be happy when it starts and a little bit sad when it's over. When you drag your baggage onto the field, you ruin the experience for you and also for your teammates.

You need to develop an on-off switch for your soccer life. You need to compartmentalize soccer as the part of your day that remains immune to all of the other stresses that might happen to consume you on any given day. If you don't, you're going to cheat yourself out of a big part of the college soccer experience and you're going to negatively impact the entire culture.

You're not going to play soccer forever. Chances are these are the last four meaningful years of soccer that you will ever experience. Protect them! Don't waste a single day of them by allowing personal issues to contaminate your soccer. It's just not worth it.

When it's time for soccer, leave your baggage at the door.

55

Exit Strategy

As important as it is to leave your baggage off the soccer field, it's equally important to leave your soccer on the soccer field.

As a college soccer player, you compete against your best friends and your roommates every day. Some days you'll beat them and some days they'll beat you and sometimes it'll probably get a little bit heated and when practice ends, your pot will still be boiling. You know what? That's fabulous! That's what soccer should be! What makes soccer worthwhile and memorable is all the emotion that it brings out of you. Imagine if soccer didn't do that. Imagine if it never made your heart race or it never made you jump in celebration or cry in defeat. If it never did any of those things, would you love it so much? Of course not! It would be about as satisfying as cooking a reasonably good omelette.

In a strong soccer culture, the players compete and they compete to the utmost of their abilities day in and day out and they battle their teammates with the same conviction as they would battle their opponents. That's how it's supposed to work. And when it does, sometimes nerves will get a little bit frayed.

When soccer is over, it's over. Don't take your individual battles back to your car or back to your dorm room. Again, you've got to compartmentalize soccer to keep it from dripping into your non-soccer world.

You want my advice? At the end of practice, if there's a teammate who really pushed your buttons, go shake her hand. Look her in the eye, shake her hand and tell her, *"Great job!"* It might seem strange to you and it will probably seem even stranger to her, but as soon as you do that, you're going to feel all of that anger drain right out of your body and you'll be able to move on with the rest of your day as the happy, socially well-adjusted person I know you to be.

When you take soccer home with you, it's a catalyst to backstabbing, and we've already discussed what a disaster that can be. That's why it's so important that you leave your soccer where it belongs – on the soccer field.

56

The Big No-No

Your teammates are going to have boyfriends or girlfriends and some of those significant others are going to be significantly good-looking. I'm sure you know where I'm heading with this and believe me, this is a line that you don't want to cross.

I don't care how good-looking that person is and I don't care how much your heart yearns for him or her, stay the heck away! Show me a college team in turmoil and I'll show you a love triangle because one teammate couldn't stay away from another teammate's boyfriend/girlfriend.

When one of these situations arises, it fractures the team because the other players are backed into taking sides. When the lines are drawn and sides are chosen, you've got feuding, in-fighting and a chemical disaster, and the healing can literally take years. You'll lose friends and gain enemies and a day or two later you'll realize what an enormous mistake you've made and how you'd give up a limb to turn back the clock and make a better decision. This is one of those topics where you can believe me now or believe me later, but eventually you will believe me.

Very few of life's issues are as clear cut, black and white as this one. When I say that your teammate's significant others are off limits, I mean 100%, lookie-no-touchy, turn and walk the other way, no questions asked, OFF LIMITS!

57

Being A Teammate

We were playing a match with some pretty heavy postseason implications. Our team was blessed with a very talented freshman midfielder who, on this night, because of her ability, may as well have been wearing a bulls-eye on her jersey. The opponent had clearly decided to target her, and they kicked her every chance they got. Early in the second half, our midfielder got tangled up with an opposing player who basically wrapped her in a headlock and slammed her to the ground. As soon as that opponent got back to her feet, our left back, Nikki, ran in and gave the opponent a pretty good two-handed shove that sent her back to the ground. It was a risky move. It could've gotten Nikki kicked out of the game. So... why did she do it?

Because that's what teammates do. They protect their own.

Being a teammate can be boiled down to one very simple phrase, a phrase that might just be my most favorite one of all: *I've got your back.*

The second-greatest gift of being part of a team is in knowing that your teammates have your back. The greatest gift is the opportunity to also have theirs.

Yes, there is strength in numbers, but that strength is magnified by a common bond born of the shared misery of giving oneself over to the greater good. As a team, you can have power! As a team, you are much stronger than any one person standing alone. And as a team, you can stand shoulder to shoulder to fight for that in which you believe. It is a bond like nothing else you will ever again experience, and my advice to you is to squeeze that orange for every drop of juice it has to offer.

As a rookie, your willingness to have backs can fast-track you into the team's social fabric, because if you have their backs, they'll in turn have yours. It doesn't always require something as dramatic as the example above; it could be as simple as speaking well of a teammate when she isn't in the room. It could be helping a teammate bag the balls when it isn't your turn. It could be giving up your window seat on an airplane. Let me give you another example that you'll most certainly have the opportunity to capitalize upon.

Preseason is a physically and emotionally grueling time, and because it is, you and your teammates will experience the deepest sleep you've ever known. And I guarantee you that if you and all your rookie classmates don't make an arrangement to look after one another, someone is going to sleep through a training session. Believe me it will happen.

When you rise from that bed, make sure your roommates are up; then go make sure the other rookies are up. Don't leave that dorm until your entire class is accounted for. And if one of your teammates can't seem to pull herself from the covers, dump a bucket of cold water on her head. She might scream bloody murder, but she'll be thanking you for years to come.

Having backs comes in many forms and fashions. It's really just about making your teammates' lives better. It's about being unselfish and letting someone else have the first shower, or picking up the equipment when it's not your turn. It's about deflecting the praise onto your teammates when the student newspaper reporter asks you about your game-winning goal. It's about showing everyone that you don't stand above the team, but that you stand with it.

When Nikki shoved that opponent, she was making a statement that if you mess with one of us, you'll have to answer to all of us. She took a physical risk by engaging that opponent, but she took that risk because of the faith she had in her teammates to protect her the way she was protecting one of her own. Isn't that the same sense of camaraderie we'd all love to experience in our own teams?

To have great teammates, you must first be a great teammate. When you give yourself to the team, the team will then give itself to you.

SECTION 6
OTHER HELPFUL
HINTS

58

The End-Of-Year Meeting

When your season ends, the coach is probably going to arrange for individual meetings with the players. This is an excellent opportunity for you to figure out exactly what you need to focus on in the spring, and where you fit into the plans for the following season.

Give this meeting the respect it deserves. First of all, don't be late. Put a reminder in your phone or write a note on your hand; do whatever you have to do, but get there on time.

In this meeting your coach is going to ask you for your thoughts on the season. He's going to ask you what you think you did well. And he's going to ask you where you think you need to improve. Then he'll tell you how he would answer all those questions.

This meeting won't be horribly dramatic, but it's a good idea to have some idea of how you're going to answer those questions because it shows that you actually take the time to think about the game and evaluate your performances.

Additionally, I suggest that you bring along a pad and a pen. It will send the message that you're taking this meeting seriously, and that will impress your coach. More importantly, when the coach tells you what he'd like you to work on, you won't have to worry about forgetting those things if you write them down.

A lot of players just breeze through these meetings without giving them much thought, which is unfortunate because this meeting is your springboard into your second semester of college soccer. Use it to clarify your training objectives so you have the best possible chance of getting or staying on the field as a sophomore. Find out exactly what he needs from you. Again he'll feed you the answers. And again you have to be smart enough to realize that.

Incidentally, if your plan is to transfer and you haven't yet told your coach, tell him now. Politely express the reasons why you'd like to transfer and ask for his assistance in speaking with other universities. By that same token, if you feel that your performance warrants an increase in scholarship money, this would be the appropriate time to broach that topic.

59

The Alums

There's a pretty good chance that at some point during the year you're going to encounter some type of alumni function. A bunch of people who look like they might have once been athletic are going to descend upon your program for a weekend and do whatever the heck they feel like doing. Meet your soccer alumni.

One weekend a year they get to come to town and tell everyone how much harder it was back when they played and how soft the current players have gotten. Don't worry about it. Fifteen years from now you'll be doing the same thing. These alums built what you walked into. They've earned a voice. And most importantly, their presence shows that they care about the program and that they want to stay connected.

Some players dread alumni functions. Let me tell you something; those players are idiots. Those players are blind to the opportunities that these alums can provide. If a 35-year-old is coming back to your university to kick around a soccer ball, it's only because she is passionate about the university and the soccer program. And that, my dear rookie, is a person that you want to know!

A well-organized alumni association is a thing of beauty. It's like the team-after-the-team. But instead of getting together to kick around a soccer ball, you get together to take vacations and find jobs and start businesses and plan weddings and raise money when there's been an emergency. When you graduate from college, very few of your teammates or classmates will be in much of a position to help you. They'll still be young and looking to find their own stride. They won't have many connections in the real world. Your alums on the other hand, well a lot of them are settled into great jobs and have a million connections and the one thing they desperately long to do is to help other soccer players from their university. I'm not making this stuff up! Your soccer alums can be some of the most powerful allies you'll ever know, but only if you actually get to know them.

You'll be a college soccer player for just four years, but you'll be a soccer alum for the rest of your life. When your alumni function rolls around, don't sit in a corner being afraid of the old people and looking to skip out at the first chance. They're not actually zombies. Introduce yourself with a smile and ask what the soccer program was like back in the old days. They'll be happy to share their war stories with you. Those alums will latch on to you and they will remember you and they will look forward to staying in touch with you and when that happens, something good just happened to you.

60

Horizons

Y ou're going to blaze your own trail through college. You're going to make your own choices and set your own boundaries and learn from your own mistakes and in the end, all of those things both good and bad will make up the best years of your life. While you're navigating your way through this bold new world, heed this simple piece of advice: Be more than an athlete.

Outside of your classes, athletics is going to consume the lion's share of your time. You're going to spend most of your time surrounded by athletes. You'll probably live with them, eat with them and hang out with them. There's nothing inherently wrong with that. However, there's a great big other world beyond the athletes and I highly recommend that you avail yourself of this other world.

College offers you opportunities that you won't get anywhere else. You can take a kick-boxing class on Monday and host your own radio show on Tuesday and volunteer at the soup kitchen on Wednesday and star in a play on Thursday! College gives you your one real chance to dabble in a zillion different activities and to bounce around from one interest to the next with no real strings attached. College gives you the chance to socialize with people that you would never associate with outside of the bubble. Embrace this! Spend some time with the freaks and the hippies and the nerds and the artsy folks that hang out in the coffee houses. Take advantage of all of this because the moment you put on that cap and gown, the bubble bursts and the honeymoon is over and you are officially a member of the real world and your days will revolve around whichever activity pays the bills.

Take advantage of the things and the people that college offers that exist in a world beyond athletics. Don't leave college filled with regret saying, *"I wish I'd done this and I wish I'd done that."* College gives you this amazing opportunity to do this, that and a hundred other things if only you make the effort to get involved.

You have a four-year window of opportunity to fill with unbelievable life experiences. Leave college with something more than just the experience of being an athlete. You'll never regret it.

61

Academics

The day will come when college is over and you're going to want (check that... need) a job. The problem is that it can be very difficult to get an interview because you don't have any experience; but how can you ever get experience when no one will give you a job? It's the hamster wheel that college grads have been spinning since the beginning of time. But since you want to eat and pay your rent and put gas in your car, you have no choice but to keep grinding. You keep sending out resumes and knocking on doors until one day, you strike potential gold!

You find a firm that is willing to let you get your foot in the door with an interview. The leadership of this firm is pretty open-minded about giving college kids with no experience a chance to come aboard and learn as they go, but they're not willing to hire just anyone. They want an office full of the best and the brightest! They understand that you're too young to have any actual real-world experience, so they're going to judge you on the one measurable body of work you do have, and it's called your GPA. And at that moment, you'll either be thankful that you focused on your academics or regretful that you did not.

I hope that is all the reason you need to remember that your academics actually are important, and it starts in your freshman year.

62

Love What You Do

College soccer will be one of the most fantastic and memorable experiences of your life… if you let it. But as I said in the very beginning, once it's gone, it's gone forever.

You've read this book for advice on surviving your rookie season. Now, here is the most important advice of all: Don't just dabble in soccer. Don't just dip your toes in the water. Dive in head-first and give yourself entirely over to the experience! Commit your entire being to the sport and to the team and soak up all that college soccer has to offer.

Love being a college soccer player. Love all of it! Love the games and the road trips and the hours stuck on busses and vans and the fancy team meals and the awful box lunches. Love the days when you train in the blistering sun and in the pouring rain. Love the shiny uniforms and the smelly locker rooms and the balls of newspaper you stuff inside your wet shoes. Love playing in the empty parks and the full stadiums. Love the pain of preseason and the nights packed in ice and the pride of finishing that one last repetition that you thought would kill you. Love the aching, burning, screaming in your legs on a fitness day. Love the heartbreak of a last minute loss and the joy of a win in overtime. Love your teammates and their selflessness and courage and their habits that annoy you and their music that you can't stand. Love the fans that support you and the coaches that drive you. Don't just exist at soccer; love it!

Give your very best to college soccer and it will repay you a hundred times over. You've got this one last chance to be a part of a team that will forever remain truly special to you. You've got four years to be your very best soccer self. Don't spend three of those years giving something less than your best and then scrambling to make amends during your senior year. You'll never regret what you gave to soccer; you'll only regret what you didn't give.

As a college soccer player you'll play roughly 80-90 games. That's all. That's all the meaningful soccer you have left. When your career finishes, make sure that you aren't left regretting a single one of those games. Make sure that you are left with a clear conscience about the effort you gave and the teammate you were each and every day.

Congratulations! Your fantastic adventure is about to begin. You may be just a rookie, but your time is now. Show the world that you are up to this challenge. This is your time to show everyone exactly what you're made of. In other words, Rookie… Get some!

A FINAL WORD

T hank you for buying my book! I know it's pretty skinny, but I hope that you feel you've gotten your money's worth.

ROOKIE is my way of giving something back to this game that has given so much to me, particularly a wealth of treasured relationships that I will forever cherish. Believe me, I'm acutely aware that a player reading this book today may be my opponent tomorrow. That's all good and well. I want every player to have a college soccer experience that is rewarding and memorable and filled with amazing adventures! I guess what I'm trying to say is that you've just been given a lot of really good advice. Please use it to your advantage.

If you feel you've gotten your money's worth from ROOKIE, I would be honored if you would take 30 seconds to leave me a five-star review on Amazon. That's the best gift you can possibly give an author. It'll take almost none of your time but it will mean the world to me. Thank you in advance!

I'd like to thank my good friends Rob Marino, Paul Denfeld and Rachael Lehner, and my wife, Beth, for their work as editors!

In a few pages you'll be able to read a chapter from my Amazon best-seller, Soccer iQ. If you're serious about becoming a better soccer player, I hope you'll consider buying it. There's no other book on the market quite like it, and I mean that sincerely.

As for ROOKIE, I'm inviting you to participate in a little experiment. I'd love to hear about any moments during your rookie season that reminded you of this book, particularly if it helped to steer you in the right direction. So, if you'd like to tell the world how this book positively impacted your rookie campaign, send me your story and I'll post it on my blog at www.soccerpoet.com. Feel free to include pictures! And if you don't want me to post your story publicly, I'd still love to hear it! Just send your story or any other feedback to coach@soccerpoet.com.

I invite you to read my blog at www.soccerpoet.com and to be my Twitter friend: @soccerpoet.

A SAMPLE CHAPTER FROM SOCCER iQ by Dan Blank

THE HOLY GRAIL

Let's begin at the beginning. Speed of play. It's the Holy Grail of soccer. Understanding this is the preeminent prerequisite for becoming a smart player. Don't question why. Fast is better than slow. That's just how it is. Your job is to take everything you can already do and do it faster.

If you can embrace the idea that fast is intrinsically better than slow, you're halfway home. If you can get an entire team of players to embrace that idea, you're going to win a lot of games.

All other things being equal, if I can get the ball from Point A to Point B with one touch, it is better than getting it there in two touches. Why? Because one touch is faster than two touches, and fast is better than slow. Yes, there are exceptions and I understand that. However, too often you play as if the exception was the rule. Let me give you some wonderful advice:

- If you can get the job done with one touch, don't take two.
- If you can get it done with two touches, don't take three.

The more touches it takes you to do your job, the slower your job gets done. The challenge for an intelligent player is to do the most effective job possible in as few touches as possible. If you could take a time machine back to your last game, could you accomplish everything that you'd accomplished during that game, but with fewer touches? It would require you to think faster. It would require you to make decisions before the ball arrived. It would require you to perform with sharper technical ability. In short, it would require you to do the things that a better player would do.

Too many players don't understand the intrinsic value of moving the ball quickly. Instead of playing a quick and simple pass that will dictate a fast tempo, the simple pass becomes their last resort – after they have evaluated and exhausted all other options. Too often they feel obligated to make an impact on the score-line every time the ball is at their feet. Every time the ball finds them, they're searching to find that killer pass; trying to figure out how to win the game right then and there. And because the answer isn't always ready to reveal itself, they get caught hemming and hawing over their options as their team's speed of play methodically dies a slow death.

Slow play is the enemy. Slow play allows your opponent to get organized. Slow play leads to turnovers. Slow play loses games.

Every pass you make doesn't have to be *the* pass. *YOU* don't have to win the game every time *YOU* touch the ball. Sometimes just moving the ball to a teammate is good enough. And moving it quickly is better than moving it slowly.

Have you seen Barcelona play? A Barcelona player will never be accused of trying to win the game each time he touches the ball – not even the prolific goal-scorer Lionel Messi. Barca's players are so patient in possession that at times they don't seem to even realize there's a goal on the field. It can look like they are just passing for passing's sake. The way they meticulously grind teams into the ground with possession has been dubbed *death by a thousand passes*. But even with all that big-picture patience, they still move the ball very quickly with a minimum of touches. So while the whole machine might be perceived as slow or deliberate, the parts are still moving at breakneck speed. Patience and speed are coexisting in stunning harmony. Barcelona's players have bought into this concept. Each player understands the value of moving the ball quickly; and each player knows that if he doesn't have the answer when the ball gets to his feet, the teammate he passes to just might. At Barcelona, speed of play is the culture.

It will also behoove you to understand soccer's speed ladder:

- Slowest – A player dribbling the ball while making lateral movements and fakes.
- Slow – A player running with the ball, straight ahead, at top speed.

- Faster – A player running without the ball
- Fastest – A moving ball

Nothing on the soccer field is faster than a moving ball. Nothing. The fastest player on the field cannot cover ten yards as fast as a kicked ball. Neither can you. And this is where you have to make a choice between taking superfluous touches that accomplish nothing more than momentarily indulging your ego... and winning. If you want to move the ball twenty yards, you'll be able to do it much faster if you pass it rather than dribble it. And fast is better than slow.

Let me add this invaluable tidbit of wisdom: To play fast, you have to *want* to play fast. It is a decision you have to make before the game begins. You've got to consciously decide to play fast. You've got to consciously decide to limit your touches. Playing fast doesn't happen by accident. It's not going to happen unless you actually decide to make it happen.

Speed of play is more than a habit – it's a lifestyle. And you can't live it until you internalize and embrace the concept that nothing is more important than speed of play. Fast is better than slow. Speed of play is what wins games. Smart players prioritize playing quickly.

Note for Coaches: It's amazing how well our team can play when we apply a one-touch restriction to a training exercise. It can be a glorious sight when our players ping the ball around at breakneck speed. The challenge for coaches is getting the players to translate that same speed of play to a match when there are no restrictions. If there is a significant difference in those two environments, then your players haven't internalized the importance of playing fast for its own sake. You've got to convince your players to *want* to play fast.

In Chapter 8 you'll read about one of my favorite possession games, called 31. It is an excellent exercise for helping players decipher when to play with one touch and when to hold the ball.

OTHER BOOKS BY DAN BLANK

Soccer iQ Volume 1 — The Amazon best-seller and an NSCAA Soccer Journal Top 5 Book of the Year.

Soccer iQ Volume 2 — More simple and effective strategies for becoming a smarter soccer player. (All the great stuff I forgot to include in Volume 1!)

HAPPY FEET — *How to Be a Gold Star Soccer Parent (Everything the Coach, the Ref and Your Kid Want You to Know)* — The best gift you can give a soccer parent! This book includes free companion videos to explain some of soccer's more mysterious concepts such as the advantage rule, offside, soccer systems and combination play. It also explains the most common errors that well-meaning soccer parents make without even realizing it.

Everything Your Coach Never Told You Because You're a Girl — This is what your coaches would have said to you if you were a boy, told through the story of a small-college team that won more games than it ever had a right to win. It's a straightforward look at the qualities that define the most competitive females. Available in 2014.

ABOUT THE AUTHOR

Dan Blank is the author of the Amazon bestseller, *Soccer iQ*, and has been coaching college soccer for over twenty years. He is the first coach in Southeastern Conference history to lead the conference's best defense in consecutive years at different universities (Ole Miss 2009, Georgia 2010). He has an 'A' License from the USSF and an Advanced National Diploma from the NSCAA. You can buy his books and read his blog at www.soccerpoet.com.

Made in the USA
Lexington, KY
13 August 2014